THE LIGHT
BEYOND THE
DARKNESS

TURNING PAIN INTO PURPOSE, A JOURNEY TO HEALING AND HOPE (A MEMOIR)

E J MARSH

BOOKS TO INSPIRE: SHAPING FUTURES

DEDICATION

This book is in honour of the most important person who's been the most influential figure in my life – that's you Mom. Your love echoes louder than crashing thunder, speaking to the deepest parts of my heart and soul every single day. Stronger than storms, it roots itself into the fabric of my existence, keeping me steady and grounded no matter what comes my way.

You've always made your best efforts to guide me through life with a presence that is constant and unwavering, even when I didn't always listen especially when the world around me felt chaotic.

Through your struggles, you've taught me resilience, courage, and compassion, even in the smallest of moments.

The laughter we've always shared reminds me of the light that shines within, and your wisdom continues to shape who I am today. I remember the time we were both on a flight to Dublin, and just as the plane was about to take off, you shouted something so unexpected it had everyone including the catholic priest sitting adjacent to us laughing. That's you, mum – finding humour in every moment and making sure no one ever forgot it.

The melody of Bobby's Girl continuously plays in my mind—and always will—a gentle reminder of the joy and memories we've always held close.

Your love, your kindness, your courage, your strength—and yes, even your imperfections—have always made you beautifully human and endlessly inspiring. You are and will always be a part of every breath I take and every step forward I make.

This book, this journey, reflects your love and the lessons you've always given me. It's a testament to the light you've always brought to my life, even in the darkest of times. It's not just a book; it's a way to honour the values and strength you've always instilled in me and continue to instil in me today.

Mum, you always keep me focused. You've kept me strong. You've saved my life in every single way.

The lessons I've learned throughout my life and the ones you've taught me have made me the person I am today. For that, I thank you and love you with all my heart and every part of my soul. I will constantly carry your love with me – always.

Through this journey, I hope I've always made you proud.

With all my love and gratitude,

Teddy xxx

Contents

PREFACE

This isn't just a story—it's a mirror.

The Light Beyond the Darkness is not about reading passively or watching someone else's life unfold from a distance. It's about stepping into the shoes of another, feeling their pain, their triumphs, their fears—and then turning that gaze inward.

This book doesn't begin with comfort. It begins in the chaos, where shadows suffocate, guilt consumes, and hope feels like a lie we tell ourselves to make it through another day. It's a place I've known well. But it's also a place I had to leave behind.

TJ's journey isn't a polished tale tied up with neat conclusions. It's raw, messy, and brutally honest. Through mental health issues, addiction, guilt, and fractured relationships, this memoir uncovers not just the darkness but the resilience it takes to claw your way out. It's not a clean escape; it's a fight. And in every fight, there's something universal—a truth about what it means to be human.

But here's where this book stands apart: it's not just about me. It's about you.

Have you ever questioned who you are at your core? Wondered why your past still pulls at you? Or doubted if you'll ever break free from the mistakes that haunt you? This book invites you to ask those questions—not to torment yourself, but to find clarity, purpose, and a way forward.

As you read, you won't just walk alongside TJ. You'll be asked to confront your own shadows. To explore the spaces in your life where healing needs to take root. To reflect on your own strength and the lessons you've learned along the way.

This isn't a story about perfection. It's about persistence. It's about taking that first uncertain step toward redemption, even when the way forward is unclear. It's about finding the courage to face your past, own your choices, and believe that healing is possible—even for you.

I won't tell you what to feel or how this ends. That's for you to discover. But I will promise you this: every page is real. Every emotion, every struggle, every flicker of hope has been lived.

So I invite you—no, I challenge you—to read this not as a bystander but as someone willing to engage. Engage with the words, engage with the emotions, and most importantly, engage with yourself. Because this isn't just about the light beyond my darkness. It's about yours too.

With every word I've written, I hope you find not just my story but your own strength, your own courage, and your own way forward. Let's take this journey together.

With love and resilience,

E.J. Marsh

WITHIN THESE WALLS

I t's absolutely freezing in Tea Jay's house; the atmosphere is cold, and the air feels icy and unapproachable. Beyond the obvious tension, you can see the vapor leaving their lips as they breathe. Tea Jay and his family have to wear jumpers over their pyjamas in bed just to keep warm.

Looking out of the window, Tea Jay sees Daffy, one of their crazy swans, going wild at a car driving by. "Shut up, stupid duck!" Tea Jay shouts through the window.

Suddenly, Tea Jay freezes, his body going ice-cold with fear as he wets himself. He mumbles to himself as he hears his mother shouting at the top of her voice.

"I want Nanny and Uncle Rob because I'm scared!"

"You bastard, you one-eyed bastard! I'm going to kill you. It's your fault, you bastard! Why, bastard? Why?" Elizabeth screams again and again.

Tea Jay clings to his frightened sister, Lacey, as they both start mumbling over and over.

"I'm frightened; I want Nanny," Lacey thinks to herself.

There's a familiar, frightening feeling in the air for young Tea Jay and his siblings—something bad is going to happen. He and his sister decide to hide under their mother's bed.

Tea Jay has very deep ocean-blue eyes and a mauve complexion. His white-blond hair reaches the base of his neck. He has a normal build for a child his age and is very pleasant to be around. He constantly tries to sleep with his mother because he has terrible nightmares, often waking up in terror, unable to sleep alone.

His mother, Elizabeth, has a reasonably sized double bedroom overlooking the back garden. White nets and cream floral-patterned curtains, with a tear at the bottom where Trixie, their dog, chewed them, dress the windows. The walls are decorated with thick, cream and beige striped wallpaper. The carpet is fiery in colour, thin, with no underlay, making it painful to walk on as the loose floorboards and sharp nails poke through. A double bed with two thick cream and beige blankets is to the left as you enter the room.

There's a picture on his mother's wall on the right—a little blonde boy with a short back-and-sides hairstyle, looking happy in blue shorts and a white t-shirt. He is hugging an older lady, maybe in her fifties, with kind green eyes, a bronze tan, and a warm smile. She wears a cream and brown blouse, a yellow dress, and sensible white walking shoes. They appear to be on a busy pier on a sunny day, looking carefree, perhaps the boy's grandmother.

Trixie, a pale grey Whippet with almost white fur, has a penchant for chewing anything she can get her teeth into. She barks at everything—anything or anyone—and will bolt out of the house at the first opportunity. The family has to be extremely cautious, as the roads in their area are treacherously busy.

The back garden is quite large, with a slabbed path running down the centre. Unsteady steps lead up to this path, just a few feet from the back door. On either side, patches of unkempt grass grow wild. A pen for the three swans, which their father stole from the park, dominates the garden. These swans are loud, always causing a ruckus. The garden gate opens onto a bustling side road, with a wooden fence that barely shields them from the prying eyes of passers-by's.

Suddenly, Tea Jay's mother's bedroom door bursts open with such force that it tears the carpet. Tea Jay and Lacey remain hidden under the bed, trembling in fear that their mother might lash out at them.

"It's your fault, it's your fault, why, why, why?" Elizabeth screams hysterically, her voice cracking under the strain.

Tears stream down her pale, exhausted face as she stands there, completely broken. Her cries intensify, soaking through her white blouse as it clings to her damp skin. The anguish in her expression is undeniable; she is shattered. Eventually, she collapses onto the bed, a sobbing heap, overcome by despair.

The neighbours, alarmed by the commotion, knock on the door, but there is no response. They quickly call the police, who arrive with a social worker in tow.

Elizabeth, standing at just over five feet tall, is thick-set, with brown eyes and pale skin. The scent of her No. 6 cigarettes mingles with the strong odour of booze that seems to cling to her. As she rocks back and forth, her bloodshot eyes stare blankly, distant and full of darkness.

Her brother opens the front door, and Elizabeth's screaming only intensifies, unable to comprehend the events that have just unfolded. The social worker attempts to console her, but it's clear that Elizabeth is in the throes of another breakdown.

"Poor woman's having another breakdown," one of the neighbours mutters to themselves.

Again and again, Elizabeth screams, "You evil, evil bastard! Your whole family is evil, you make me sick, you one-eyed bastard. Die, bastard, die!"

"Please don't cry, Mommy," Tea Jay whispers, his small voice quivering with fear.

"He's gone, I've lost him," Elizabeth sobs hysterically.

"You're too young to understand, Tea Jay. One day you will, I promise," she says, trying to reassure her terrified son.

"Why do you smell funny, Mommy? Where's Daddy?" Tea Jay asks, his voice tinged with sadness.

"It doesn't matter, son!" she cries out, dismissing his concerns.

"What's in that bottle you're drinking, Mommy? It smells funny," Tea Jay asks, his curiosity untainted by his confusion.

"It's just Mommy's medicine, don't worry. Mommy's okay," she says, her voice shaky but attempting to be soothing.

Mrs. Sikes, the family social worker, eventually manages to calm Elizabeth down in the kitchen, offering comfort and trying to console her.

The kitchen is modest in size, with a square woodchip table covered in an adhesive sheen finish. Two plain glass windows look out onto the green, filling the room with a dull light. The kitchen connects to a short hallway leading to the front door, directly opposite Uncle Rich's bedroom. The walls are painted cream, with a picture of three ducks adorning the space opposite the windows. A vintage print of J.H. Lynch's "Tina" hangs on the wall by the hallway entrance, facing the cooker and cupboards.

Outside, the green is a large patch of grass where Tea Jay and his brother often sit. It's a place for them and the local kids to play when they're allowed out.

"Are you going to be alright, Elizabeth?" Mrs. Sikes asks, her tone laced with concern.

"This is no place for three innocent children. I don't want to take them into care, but I will if I have to," the social worker thinks grimly.

"I'm sorry I've caused all this commotion; I just can't cope without my husband," Elizabeth cries out, the weight of her words heavy in the room.

"Are you going to harm yourself, Elizabeth? More importantly, are your children safe if we leave?" the police officer asks, her concern evident.

"Timewaster! Can't she see that she has three innocent children? We have more important calls to attend to," the officer thinks impatiently.

"I'd never harm my pissing kids—they're all I've got," Elizabeth blurts out, her sorrow overwhelming her.

"I'll call in on you next week, okay, Elizabeth?" the social worker says, trying to offer some reassurance.

The family lives in a four-bedroom semi-detached house in the West Midlands. A small flat roof tops a brick shed outside the front door. A wooden gate, with a latch that barely works, guards the entrance. Two back gardens sit to the left of the green, and to the right, there are eight terraced houses, their backyards facing the alleyway that separates them.

A couple of weeks later, Elizabeth seems to have calmed down. However, her personality remains a volatile mix of Jekyll and Hyde. The doctor has prescribed her tranquilizers to help manage her moods.

"Come on, you three, breakfast," their mother calls through the living room door.

"Coming, Mom," Tea Jay responds.

"Lacey, eat that porridge now; do you hear me, lady?" her mother snapped, her voice rising with frustration.

Lacey, her eyes wide with fear, pushed the porridge around her bowl, her little hands shaking as she hesitated. Elizabeth's patience snapped in an instant. With an exaggerated motion, she grabbed Lacey's face and shoved it down into the porridge, as though the breakfast was suddenly the most important thing in the world.

Porridge flew everywhere—in great, messy splatters across the table, all over Tea Jay and Jason, and into Lacey's hair and face. For a brief, absurd moment, it felt like a ridiculous, chaotic breakfast comedy sketch, but the room was too tense for anyone to laugh.

Tea Jay wiped a glob of porridge from his face, his heart pounding in his chest. "Mommy, why did you do that?" he asked, his voice trembling, not sure whether to cry or laugh.

"Shut your mouth, Tea Jay, or you'll get the same!" she screams, her eyes wild with fury.

Tea Jay recoils, frightened and unsure. The words sting, but the fear grips him even tighter. Almost as quickly as the rage came, it begins to fade. Elizabeth takes a breath, her face softening, regret settling in. "Ahh, come here, Lacey. I'm sorry, I'm sorry," she murmurs, pulling her little girl close. Lacey, still teary-eyed, leans into her mother's embrace. The pain remains, though soothed for now.

"Never mind, I'll treat you all to ice cream when we go uptown," Elizabeth adds, her voice taking on a lighter tone as if that could erase the tension. "Come on now, hurry up, or we'll miss the bus. We're meeting Nanny at her stall in the market."

Later that afternoon, Lacey is playing with some rubbish she's found on the floor, oblivious to her mother's repeated warnings.

"Lacey! Put that rubbish down now, or I'll tan your backside black and blue! Do you hear me, lady?" Elizabeth snaps, her patience hanging by a thread. "I won't tell you again. Hand it over."

Just then, something catches her eye. Elizabeth's face changes instantly, her voice dropping to a near whisper. "Oh my God... Come on, quick, we're going home!" she says, her tone urgent, no room for argument.

"But Mommy, you said we'd get ice cream," Jason protests, confused by the sudden shift.

"I'll buy you two ice creams each if you just shut up and move! Come on, quick!" Elizabeth's voice lifts with excitement now, practically dragging them along.

Back home that evening, the phone rings.

"Mom... the phone's ringing," Jason calls out.

"Well, answer it and ask who it is! I'm busy!" Elizabeth shouts back.

"It's Nanny, Mom," Jason yells up the stairs.

Louise, Elizabeth's mother, has kind, gentle brown eyes that seem to know too much. Her curly grey hair frames her round face, and she always wears the same blue flowery blouse and long, colourful skirt. The familiar scent of her perfume lingers, soft and comforting.

"Elizabeth, are you alright? I've been worried," Nanny's voice is lined with concern.

"Sorry, Mom. I had to get the kids home quick today. Sorry I didn't meet you at the market," Elizabeth replies, her voice strained, though trying to sound casual.

"What's going on, Liz? You haven't been drinking again, have you?" Nanny's suspicion is clear, her tone sharper now.

"No, Mother!" Elizabeth snaps, defensive. "It's just Lacey. You know how she picks up anything off the floor."

"Yes, but what's that got to do with making me wait and miss my bus, Elizabeth?" Nanny demands, her voice growing more impatient.

"Well, Lacey must have picked up someone's takings from one of the market stalls. There's over £700 here, Mom," Elizabeth says, now laughing, disbelief in her voice. "Looks like Christmas is sorted this year!"

"Elizabeth!" Nanny gasps, her tone dropping in shock and fear. "Oh, good God, Elizabeth... That's stealing! I didn't raise you like this. You're thirty-three years old, with three kids to think about. Do you want to end up in prison?"

"Don't be daft, Mother!" Elizabeth laughs, brushing off the concern. "Michael was always on the rob and only ended up inside once. Besides, it was Lacey who found it. What are you saying? She's going to end up in the nick too?"

Nanny mutters under her breath, her anger growing. "Michael. That bloody bastard. He's to blame for you turning out like this."

"Leave Michael out of this!" Elizabeth snaps again, her patience wearing thin.

"Anyway, Mother, that's the market's fault for not looking after their cash. I'm not giving that money back, no way!" Elizabeth says, her laughter sharp.

Nanny sighs deeply. "Well, don't say I didn't warn you."

Later that evening, Tea Jay, still feeling uneasy, goes to his mother.

"Mommy, it's really cold in my room. Can I sleep with you? Please, Mommy," Tea Jay pleads, his voice small and trembling.

"No," she snaps quickly. "You're four now. You have to learn to sleep on your own. I'm going over to the club, and your Uncle Rich will be watching you all."

Tea Jay's stomach tightens at the mention of his uncle. "Uncle Rich?" The words leave a bad taste in his mouth, and his tummy feels funny, like when he's eaten too much candy.

"Yes, Richard!" Elizabeth repeats, already irritated. "Now, do as you're told."

Tea Jay's voice falters. "But... Mommy... I don't like Richard. He... he scares me."

Elizabeth softens, noticing his distress. "What's the matter with you? What's Richard done?"

Tea Jay opens his mouth to speak, but no words come out. His fear swallows him whole, making it impossible to say what's on his mind.

"Tea Jay?" Elizabeth kneels down, her anger melting. "We'll talk later, okay?"

She senses something's wrong, but the pull of a night out and a drink wins over her mother's instinct. She grabs her coat and leaves.

Later that night...

"I want to stay in Mommy's room, but she'll hit me if I wake her up," Tea Jay mumbles to himself, the words looping over and over in his head.

His room is cold and uninviting, the blue walls too dark, the single light casting harsh shadows. His teddy bears, scattered on the floor, seem more like silent witnesses than comforting companions. He clutches the biggest one tightly as if it could shield him from the fear crawling inside him.

Suddenly, a low groan echoes through the house. Tea Jay's heart races, his tiny body frozen in fear. The groan comes again, sending icy chills down his spine. Then, there's a knock on the door. Just one. Then silence. He waits, his breath shallow, listening. Another knock, this time on the window.

He's shaking now, gripping his teddy so hard his knuckles turn white. Then he sees it—a figure on the wall. Dark eyes, hollow and terrifying, staring back at him. He tries to scream, but nothing comes out. He's frozen, locked in place as the figure looms larger.

"Please don't hurt me," he thinks, his little mind crying out.

Finally, a scream rips through him just as the figure vanishes. Richard bursts through the door, his face twisted in anger.

"Get back to bed, you little fucker!" Richard shouts.

Tea Jay sobs uncontrollably, his body trembling violently. "Mommy, I want my mommy!"

"I want Mommy! I want Mommy!" Tea Jay pleads, his voice desperate and frantic.

"Your mom's over at the club! Stop screaming, or I'll give you something to scream about. You've just woke me up! You had a nightmare, didn't you?" Richard yells, frustration brewing in his voice.

"I didn't, Richard, because I saw a man on the wall," Tea Jay cries, his voice trembling with fear.

"A man on the wall? You had a nightmare," Richard scoffs.

"I didn't! There was a man on the wall; I saw him," Tea Jay insists, tears streaming down his face.

"You had a nightmare! Now go back to sleep, or you'll feel the back of my hand," Richard snaps, stomping away.

Richard stays at Elizabeth's house because he has nowhere else to go, and she needs the extra money since she's on benefits. He's about five feet nine, always smelling of stale lager and sweat. His curly black hair is messy, and his dark brown eyes are unsettling. He's got a medium build, walks funny, and is usually unshaven, wearing tatty jeans and an old leather jacket with a hole in one of the arms.

A few days later, Tea Jay is told he has to get used to being back in his own room. Fear still clings to him like a shadow, and he pleads with his mother for one more night by her side.

"Can I sleep with you, Mommy? Please? I don't want to stay in that room again. It scares me. There's a bogeyman in there," Tea Jay begs, his voice barely above a whisper, trembling with fear.

"What have I told you, Tea Jay? Come on, what have I told you?" Elizabeth yells, her voice tight with anger, the stink of alcohol clinging to her words.

Before Tea Jay can even finish his plea, his head jerks violently to the side, his mother's hand cracking loudly against his cheek. His eyes instantly well with tears, his nose running as the pain stabs through his small frame. His heart sinks, heavy with confusion and hurt, his world collapsing in that single, crushing moment.

"Mommy, please stop hitting me. I just wanted to stay in your bed because I'm scared," Tea Jay cries, his voice choked with sobs, tears streaming down his face like rivers of pain.

"Get to bed now! Or so help me, God, I'll kill you," Elizabeth screams, her fury shaking the room as Tea Jay stumbles to his bedroom, sobbing uncontrollably.

A few days later, Tea Jay tiptoes downstairs, his heart still heavy from the nights before. He finds Uncle Rob, Nanny Louise, and Mrs. Sikes, the social worker, sitting in the living room.

The living room is large but sparsely furnished. Grass-green fabric settees sit against the walls, and a 40-inch black-and-white television rests on a white gloss brick fireplace. There's a wooden sideboard with records—Elvis Presley, Max Bygrave's, and others—stacked inside.

To the left of the stairs is Richard's room, a small, cluttered space littered with empty beer cans and dirty laundry. The room reeks of stale beer, its stench seeping into the house.

"Where's Mommy?" Tea Jay asks, his voice trembling with fear and confusion.

"Mommy's very poorly, Tea Jay. She's been taken to the hospital," Uncle Rob says gently, pulling Tea Jay close to him.

"Is Mommy going to die, Uncle Rob?" Tea Jay asks, his heart clenching as he looks into Rob's eyes.

"No, Tea Jay, it's not that kind of hospital," Rob reassures him softly, lifting him up into his arms.

"You and Lacey are going on a little adventure, Tea Jay. You're both going to stay with two of your mommy's friends for a while, until she gets better," Mrs. Sikes adds, her voice gentle yet firm, trying to comfort the frightened child.

Lacey, who is a year younger than Tea Jay, looks on with wide, innocent brown eyes. Her small frame trembles, but she's quiet, holding onto her brother's hand. Lacey is petite, with a mauve complexion and a tendency to scream if she doesn't get her way.

Uncle Rob is their favourite—kind, caring, and the only one who makes them feel safe. He stands at about 5 feet 8 inches tall, with a comb-over hairstyle and soft brown eyes. He wears blue jeans and a dark t-shirt with his BT work jacket.

Tea Jay's tears fall freely as he looks from Rob to Mrs. Sikes, to Nanny Louise. His small body shakes uncontrollably with fear and confusion.

"I want Mommy... I want Lacey... Where's Mommy?" he cries out, collapsing into Rob's arms as the world around him spins in fear and uncertainty.

Tea Jay's mind drifts to one of the few places where he feels safe—his Uncle Rob's arms. Known to all the kids as the gentle giant, Rob has a way of making the chaos disappear, even if just for a moment. He often catches Tea Jay mid-run, lifting him high and spinning him upside down like a gumball. In those seconds, everything feels light, and the world doesn't seem so heavy. Rob isn't just an uncle; he's a surrogate father, always smiling, always making time for them.

BURNING FLESH

M rs. Sikes and Tea Jay's Nanny, Lou, were preparing to take him to social services. Mrs. Sikes knelt down beside the small boy, offering a soft, reassuring smile, though the weight of the moment was heavy in the air. "You'll see Lacey soon, Tea Jay. We're just going on a little trip, and Nanny will be with you the whole time."

Lou, visibly struggling to hold herself together, nodded in agreement, though her heart was breaking. The boy looked so small, so innocent, yet he was being pulled into a world that made no sense to him.

"I bet you'd like a ride in my flashy new car, wouldn't you, Tea Jay?" Mrs. Sikes added, trying to lighten the mood, her smile growing a little wider.

"Can Nanny come too?" Tea Jay's eyes were wide with worry, clutching tightly to his grandmother's hand.

"Of course she can come, sweetheart. Now, let's get going, shall we?" Mrs. Sikes replied, her smile still warm, but something in her eyes was colder than her tone.

The shiny blue Ford Escort gleamed in the driveway, and despite the dread building in his small chest, Tea Jay found himself momentarily distracted by the car—it was his favourite colour. Nanny Lou helped him with his tiny suitcase, and he gave his Uncle Rob a small wave goodbye as they prepared to leave.

"Nanny, why are you crying?" Tea Jay's soft, concerned voice broke through the stillness, his confusion clear.

Lou, wiping away a tear hastily, forced a smile. "Oh, love, it's just the dust. I'm fine, I promise. Be a good boy for Mrs. Sikes, okay? Make Nanny proud."

"Nanny, where are we going?" Tea Jay's voice trembled slightly, his small hand tightening around hers.

"Please, call me Sarah," Mrs. Sikes interjected, still with that polished smile. "We don't need to be so formal."

Lou, though barely holding herself together, managed a tight nod. "Thank you, Sarah."

Mrs. Sikes—or Sarah, as she preferred—was tall and lean, her wavy blonde hair framing her face in perfect waves. She exuded confidence, but her seemingly warm demeaner masked a certain coldness—a woman who was used to delivering bad news. As she spoke, Lou felt her stomach churn with dread.

"I know this is hard for you, Louise. But maybe, in the long run, it's best for everyone," Sarah said, her tone too matter-of-fact for Lou's liking.

Lou's response was immediate, her voice shaking with anger. "Best for everyone? What do you know about what's best for my family? That poor boy doesn't even know what's happening to him!"

Sarah blinked, taken aback by Lou's venomous outburst but maintaining her professional composure. "I understand you're upset—"

"No, you don't," Lou snapped. "Do you have children, Mrs. Sikes? Or are you too young to know anything about what it's like to be a mother? You have no idea what this is doing to my daughter, or to him!" Lou pointed at Tea Jay, whose confused eyes darted between the two women.

"I'm almost twenty-five," Sarah replied, trying to maintain control of the conversation, her voice clipped.

Lou scoffed. "Almost twenty-five? You're just a kid yourself! And yet, here you are, playing judge and jury over my family."

Sarah's smile faded slightly, replaced by a more serious expression. "Mrs. L, I understand your anger. But we need to ensure your grandchildren are safe, especially while Elizabeth is in the hospital."

Lou's temper flared again. "Hospital? My daughter isn't just in the hospital, she's had a breakdown! Her husband left her with nothing, and now this—this will kill her!"

Sarah's voice was steady, but there was a hard edge to it now. "Louise, Elizabeth was found by the police in a highly intoxicated state, abusive and violent. She assaulted an officer and had to be restrained. This isn't the first time there's been a problem."

Lou's face paled. "What are you talking about? What do you mean, this isn't the first time?"

Sarah didn't flinch. "Your daughter's drinking has been a concern for a while now. Social services have been monitoring the situation for the past year. We've had to step in several times."

Lou's eyes filled with disbelief. "I had no idea it was that bad... I didn't know."

Sarah nodded sympathetically but pushed forward. "That's why we're seeking an Interim Care Order. The court will decide whether it's safe for the children to remain in the home while Elizabeth recovers."

Lou felt the world tilt slightly beneath her. "A care order? No... You can't. She's their mother."

"I'm afraid it's the only option right now," Sarah said, her voice firm but not unkind.

Tea Jay, sensing the tension, tugged at his nanny's sleeve. "Nanny, why are you crying? Did I do something wrong?"

Lou dropped to her knees, pulling him into a tight embrace, her tears falling freely now. "No, love. You've done nothing wrong. You're my good boy."

"Nanny's just had some upsetting news. There's nothing to worry about, okay, Tea Jay?" Lou says, trying to sound reassuring, though her voice wavers slightly.

Upon arriving at the social services office, Tea Jay is led up a cold, concrete staircase from the car park. At the top of the stairs, a frosted glass window to the left obscures the view, only revealing blurry figures moving past. He's ushered into a small, sterile office on the left, filled with a few scattered children's toys and a small cream-colored two-seater sofa against the wall. The room is bare, with cold brown carpet tiles on the floor and no pictures on the walls, giving the space an unsettling feel.

"Where's Nanny?" Tea Jay asks, his voice trembling with the weight of sadness.

Noticing his nanny is no longer with him, Tea Jay becomes more distressed, his small hands gripping the edge of the sofa as he looks around, desperately hoping to see her face again.

Nanny Lou always has a warm, comforting smile, the kind that makes everything feel safe. Her hands are soft and smell faintly of flowers, and she often sings gentle nursery rhymes that makes the world seem less scary.

"Your nanny's just gone to get you some sweets, Tea Jay. She'll be back soon. Aren't you lucky?" Mrs. Sikes says, her voice warm yet rehearsed.

"I don't want sweets. I want my mommy," Tea Jay mumbles, his small voice cracking with the rising tide of tears.

"I bet I know what you'd like, Tea Jay. How about some chocolate?" Sarah suggests, trying to keep the situation calm.

But Tea Jay doesn't want chocolate. He doesn't want distractions. He wants the comfort of his mother or his nanny—someone familiar to hold onto in this strange place that feels colder than the chill in the air.

Suddenly, his eyes widen with recognition as he hears his nanny's voice from outside the door. "I want Nanny! I want my sister Lacey! She's my sister, and I love her!" Tea Jay cries out, tears spilling down his cheeks as he curls into himself in the corner of the room.

"We're going to see Lacey at Mommy's friend's house very soon. It won't be long now, I promise, Tea Jay. Is that alright?" Mrs. Sikes tries to comfort him, though her voice falters slightly under the pressure of his overwhelming sadness.

"But I want Mommy," he sobs, the words coming out louder now, his small body trembling with each breath. "I want my mommy..."

As Tea Jay's cries grow louder, they catch the attention of the manager, who enters the room, concerned. "Is everything okay, Sarah?" the man asks, casting a glance at the weeping boy curled in the corner.

"Everything's fine, Guy. This is Tea Jay, and he's just a little overwhelmed because he's going on a big adventure today, aren't you, Tea Jay?" Sarah says, trying to lighten the mood, though her voice lacks the genuine warmth it once had.

The manager, Guy, kneels down, his tone shifting to something more firm than friendly. "Come on now, Tea Jay. The sooner you get used to not having your mother around, the better off you'll be."

Tea Jay doesn't understand. He just continues to rock back and forth, the weight of the world pressing down on his little heart. The room feels cold and unwelcoming, the absence of his loved ones filling him with an indescribable dread. His small body shivers, not from the cold, but from fear.

"Want Mommy...want Mommy..." he murmurs as he rocks himself, clinging onto the only thing that gives him comfort.

Guy, growing more impatient, says sharply to Sarah, "I'll handle this one. He's just going to have to learn."

"He's only four! He's a frightened child who feels abandoned," Sarah pleads, hoping to soften Guy's approach.

"Well, he's not going to learn by being coddled. It's the mother's fault the boy is like this," Guy mutters dismissively, but finally concedes, "Alright, fine. We'll take him together."

Tea Jay is eventually taken to his new home, a large, imposing house just outside Coleshill, set against the countryside. The sprawling seven-bedroom house feels like a world away from anything he's ever known. As they arrive, Mrs. Sikes tries to explain, "This is your new home, Tea Jay, at least for now."

But Tea Jay's mind is elsewhere—lost in thoughts of his mother, his nanny, his sister. As he steps out of the car, the weight of his small suitcase in his hand feels like a chain dragging him deeper into a world that no longer makes sense.

The entrance leads to a beautiful sitting room with a lovely wood-burning fireplace. The room is decorated with calm chocolate-coloured wallpaper, and the pleasant aroma of baking wafts from the large kitchen. There's also a separate games room for the foster children who stay on occasion. The property's large garden is home to various animals, including a black collie dog that Tea Jay falls in love with immediately.

On the first floor, there are five bedrooms, including Tea Jay's, and the main bedroom where the foster parents sleep.

"Hello, Tea Jay. My name's Valerie," his foster parent says warmly.

Valerie is in her late thirties, with great manners. She's extremely polite, warm, and approachable. She has blonde hair, a petite figure, and tanned skin that doesn't require much makeup. Val takes care of her appearance, loves to go running, and bakes every Thursday. She looks very stylish and loves to hold yoga classes for her friends. She doesn't smoke or drink alcohol.

Little Tea Jay, shy and uncertain, tries to hide behind the social worker. Nevertheless, he's gently ushered into the house.

"I want Mommy," Tea Jay cries out, uncertain who to address since all these people are strangers.

Tea Jay tries to hide in the corner of the room. All he wants is to see a familiar, friendly face to reassure and comfort him. He begins to feel resentment and mistrust, becoming fearful of the people around him as he withdraws further. The broken little boy is beginning to grieve for the only family he's ever known, retreating deeper into himself.

Standing by a large staircase, Tea Jay hears a familiar voice coming from upstairs and calls out his sister's name. All of his fear suddenly disappears as he feels reassured that he's not alone and that he's going to see his little sister.

"Lacey! I want Lacey!" he calls out, but there's no reply.

He tries to climb the large winding staircase, but as he struggles with the steep stairs, the social worker quickly swoops him up into his arms.

"You and I need to have a little chat, Tea Jay," the social worker says sharply to the frustrated little boy who is desperately trying to get away.

Tea Jay struggles and manages to break free from the social worker's grip. He begins screaming his sister's name as he climbs the stairs. On the first floor, Tea Jay sees someone holding an older girl's hand who resembles his younger sister from behind. He calls out Lacey's name over and over.

"Lacey, it's me, Tea Jay, your brother!" the four-year-old cries in his young Brummagem accent as he runs up to the two girls, calling his sister's name once more.

Suddenly, the social worker quickly swoops Tea Jay up in his arms again, just before Tea Jay can see the girl's face.

"Tea Jay, there's something I need to tell you. You must listen to me, okay? Do you understand?" the social worker says softly.

Tea Jay doesn't understand; all he wants is to go back upstairs to see Lacey.

"I want Lacey, my sister," Tea Jay mumbles.

"That little girl upstairs isn't Lacey, I'm afraid. She's not here, Tea Jay. She's with another mommy and daddy," the social worker explains gently.

The little boy sinks to the floor in floods of tears.

"The lady with the blue car said I would be going on an adventure with my sister, Lacey. I'm telling my mom on you," Tea Jay cries out, his voice full of sorrow.

"You'll only be here for a few days—not long, I promise, honestly," the social worker says, trying to offer some comfort.

In the meantime, Tea Jay begins to act out with his new foster parents and struggles to settle into his new home. Within days of arriving, he gets in trouble with his foster father, Mike. Tea Jay refuses to engage with the other children, starts swearing, and even spits at the little girl he saw upstairs, causing her to run to her foster mother in floods of tears.

Mike, as he prefers to be called by his friends, is in his late forties, about five feet eight inches tall, with brownish receding hair. He has a sun-tanned complexion, hazel eyes, and a slightly unsettling, staring expression. Mike smokes a pipe and enjoys playing bowls with his wife and friends.

"Come here now, boy. I won't have you coming here and upsetting the other children. And if I ever hear you swear at anyone again, there'll be big trouble, my lad. Now get to bed, now," Mike snaps.

Tea Jay's room is on the first floor. He has a single bed against the far wall. The walls are wallpapered with a picture of two small girls playing with prams, cartoon-like characters with ginger hair. The carpet features Bambi and a Dalmatian in a park. There's a single white wardrobe in the corner of the room, along with a small white chest of drawers next to it.

There's something strange to young Tea Jay in this house: everyone is always smiling and happy.

"There's no shouting, and I don't have to see Uncle Rich, because he makes me frightened, and he does very naughty things," he thinks to himself.

Tea Jay is afraid to tell anyone because his uncle told him that if he speaks out, he'll tell the ghost to get Tea Jay. He also said that no one would believe Tea Jay because he's just a child, and everyone would think he's telling lies.

Tea Jay hears someone in the kitchen saying, "Poor child! With a mother like that, I'm not surprised he's the way he is. Bloody alcoholic, she doesn't deserve those kids."

Tea Jay hears the words but takes no notice because he doesn't understand in his young, innocent mind what they're saying or who they're talking about.

Tea Jay smells something nice coming from the kitchen and appears at the entrance where Valerie is baking bread and making a cake. She notices little Tea Jay watching her bake.

"Hello, young man! You shouldn't really be in here, you know. A kitchen can be a very dangerous place for a little boy like you. Never mind, it's okay because you're with me," Val, his foster mother, says with a smile.

The kitchen window looks out onto the garden and farmland. There are a few sheep and cows in the field in the distance. A black border collie stands just outside the window, and Val picks up Tea Jay so he can see out of the big window. He smiles at the animals, but Val can see that he's deeply troubled. She cuddles and consoles him as he cries boiling tears. However, he's not used to all this affection and is very confused. Still, he throws his little arms around her neck.

"Ahh, Tea Jay, someone likes a cuddle, don't they, young man?" Valerie says, giving him a kiss on his tearful little cheek.

"Don't worry, Tea Jay, there'll be lots of cuddles here," Valerie continues, smiling warmly down at him. "Would you like to help me make a cake?"

Tea Jay nods his head, indicating that he would.

"Well, I bake every Thursday morning. Would you like to join me?" she asks.

"Yeah," Tea Jay says softly.

"Yes, please, Mommy," his foster mother gently corrects him.

"But you're not my mommy," Tea Jay says, looking confused. "I want Mommy and Lacey," the lost little boy mumbles.

"I understand you're frightened and don't quite understand, Tea Jay. I'm not saying I'm your real mommy, because Mommy's in the hospital resting, isn't she? I'm your foster mommy. So, you've actually got two mommies, Tea Jay. Aren't you lucky?" Valerie explains kindly.

Tea Jay nods his little head, still not fully comprehending.

"Well, you've actually got two mommies now. I'm your other mommy, Tea Jay," Valerie says, trying to reassure him.

Tea Jay suddenly beams a smile up at her, and she picks him up, showering him with affection.

Over the next two or three months, Tea Jay eventually settled into his new home. He enjoyed all the attention from his new family and loved playing with the animals. One day, as he came into the house from playing with the dog, he found Mrs. Sikes sitting on the sofa talking to Mike.

"Hello, Tea Jay," Mrs. Sikes said to him.

He was confused and afraid because, in his young, impressionable mind, she told him lies and took him away from his nanny. The memories of being taken from his family flooded back, and he closed up, refusing to approach the social worker. Instead, he ran and buried his face in Mike's chest.

"Tea Jay, would you like to see Mommy?" Sarah asked him gently.

"But that's Mommy over there, making bread," Tea Jay said, looking confused.

"Okay, Tea Jay, would you like to see your other Mommy and Lacey?" Mrs. Sikes asked the very confused little boy.

A beam shot across his face as he shouted his sister's name.

"Would you like to go home and see them really soon? That will be exciting, wouldn't it, Tea Jay?" the social worker said to the excited little boy.

The following Sunday, Tea Jay was getting ready for church when he heard Valerie call out, "Come on, Tea Jay, time for church."

Tea Jay's foster parents had been visiting Elizabeth in the hospital. They'd been encouraging her to join a group they belonged to, hoping to convert her to their faith. They both felt she was fit and able to go home now.

"Tea Jay, are you excited to be going to see your family?" Valerie asked him.

Tea Jay, very confused and scared, ran with open arms to his foster mother, whom he now called "Mommy." She swooped him up in her arms, showering him with affection while shedding a few tears.

"Come on, Tea Jay, there, there; it'll be alright. You're going home, to where Mommy's all better," his foster mother said, trying to comfort the very upset, confused little boy.

"What about little Lacey? Don't you think she wants to see you?" his foster mother asked.

A week later, Tea Jay was in bed touching himself, as many children tend to do at a young age. Suddenly, he heard someone call his name. As his bedroom door flew open with force, it was clear someone had seen what he was doing.

"Oh my God, Tea Jay, that's disgusting! You evil, horrible child. Repent, repent, you disgusting child!" they screamed over and over, repeatedly slapping him about his face and head, while dragging him into the bathroom, kicking and screaming.

"Repent, you evil child; repent! Pray for forgiveness, you evil child," they continued to shout as they forced his right hand under a hot water boiler for several seconds.

Tea Jay bellowed out in pain, screaming again and again. He screamed so hard that something snapped within him. His tiny hands shook violently as he cried out, "Mommy, Mommy, Mommy!"

A huge blister formed around the back of his tiny hand and thumb. He shook uncontrollably, screaming louder and louder until he finally passed out.

When the severity of Tea Jay's injury was realized, help was called, and he was rushed to the hospital.

At the hospital, the nurses and burns specialists noticed that the skin on Tea Jay's right thumb and the back of his hand felt leathery. It was clear from their concerned looks that the damage was extensive.

After a week, the hospital delivered the grim news to Social Services: the little boy would need several operations to restore normal function to his hand. They informed Mrs. Sikes that he had sustained third-degree burns.

As Mrs. Sikes listened to the doctors over the phone, a faint unease began to build in her chest. Something about the whole situation didn't sit right with her, and as she prepared for her visit the next day, the unease grew into a knot of worry.

The following day, Mrs. Sikes visited the hospital to inquire further about how such a terrible injury could have occurred.

"What happened to the boy's hand? How could such a young child sustain such a horrific injury?" Mrs. Sikes asked the doctors. Her voice, though steady, carried a hint of disbelief.

The doctor exchanged a glance with one of the nurses before responding. "We were told that the boy tipped a cup of boiling water on himself. But..." the doctor hesitated for a moment, lowering his voice. "The woman who brought him in seemed unusually calm for someone dealing with such a severe burn. Her hands were trembling, but she didn't seem panicked."

Mrs. Sikes felt a chill run down her spine. Calm? Trembling? That didn't seem right at all. Her worry deepened, but she said nothing, deciding to hear everything before jumping to conclusions.

The doctor continued, "The matron who spoke with the woman isn't here today—she's currently on sick leave. But from what I understand, the woman claimed it was an accident." He paused, glancing at his notes. "However, the matron had noted that she found the woman's demeaner... odd."

Mrs. Sikes frowned. "Do you know when the matron will return? I'd like to speak with her directly."

The doctor shook his head. "I'm afraid not. She's the only one who had direct contact with the woman who brought Tea Jay in. Once she's back, I'm sure she could provide more clarity."

Mrs. Sikes felt the knot in her stomach tighten further. If the matron was the only one who had seen the woman, and she was on sick leave, the questions surrounding this incident may linger much longer than she anticipated. Something wasn't adding up. Who could this woman be?

"Well, the last time I saw the boy, he was almost ready to be discharged from foster care," Mrs. Sikes said, her tone now laced with suspicion. "Can I inquire who brought him into Accident and Emergency? Was it his foster parents or his natural mother?"

The doctor glanced at his notes again, but there was no clear answer. "The paperwork isn't complete, and with the matron absent, we don't have confirmation. It's possible she'll know when she's back."

As Mrs. Sikes walked away from the conversation, her thoughts raced. I've never sensed anything unusual with his foster family, she reflected, but something gnaws at me now. Her mind was unsettled, leaving her with more questions than answers.

FLAMES OF BLAME

Almost three years had passed since Tea Jay's horrific injury. Despite numerous operations to remove the damaged layers of skin from his right hand and thumb, Tea Jay still wasn't fully healed. The doctors had tried to restore the functionality of his hand, but the road to recovery was far from over. With more surgeries ahead before they could complete a skin graft, it seemed like the pain would never truly end.

While his mother spoke with his psychologist, Tea Jay played quietly outside the office with Lacey and his nanny, Lou.

"Nanny, my hand smells funny again. It smells like... poo," Tea Jay said, wrinkling his nose. His small voice trembled as he looked down at the bandaged hand that had been the source of so much pain.

Lou knelt beside him; her face heavy with concern but softened by a warm smile. "Don't worry, sweetheart. The doctors are going to make it all better when they put you to sleep again. Nanny won't let anything happen to you."

But her reassurances couldn't stop Tea Jay's tears. "I don't like the gas mask, Nanny. I don't want to go to sleep," he cried, clinging to her, his tears mingling with fear and exhaustion.

Lou fought back tears of her own as she cradled the small boy. The sight of him so vulnerable made her heart ache. "I'll be right here when you wake up," she whispered. "Nanny will be here."

Inside the psychologist's office, a different kind of fear gnawed at Tea Jay's mother, Elizabeth.

"I'm afraid I have some difficult news, Mrs. M.," the psychologist said softly, though the weight of his words hit like a blow. "The surgeries to your son's hand have been successful, physically. But psychologically... I'm afraid Tea Jay will never be the same again."

Elizabeth recoiled as though she had been struck. "What the hell do you mean? Never the same?" Her voice cracked under the strain of tears she tried to hold back. "Are you saying you know everything? Like you're God or something?"

Her anger was fierce, but beneath it was terror. Terror of losing her children. Of being blamed.

The psychologist maintained his calm, though his expression grew more serious. "How did the accident happen again, Mrs. M.?"

Elizabeth's defences went up immediately. Her mind raced, and the familiar anxiety that haunted her pushed its way to the surface. They're going to blame me. They'll take my children. She could already feel the ground beneath her crumbling.

"That bastard foster parent did it," she muttered under her breath. But there was no conviction behind her words, only the desperate grasping of a woman trying to shift blame.

"Were they arrested?" the psychologist asked, his tone neutral, probing.

Elizabeth avoided his gaze. "No. The cops and Social Services are investigating it... but they don't even know who brought my boy to the hospital in the first place."

Her voice wavered as she relayed the messy, unresolved details. "They're investigating me, too. They don't know who took him to the hospital. I've got witnesses, though—people who can vouch for where I was that day. But... it's family, so they're saying maybe I've made them lie for me." She paused, her thoughts tangling as paranoia tightened its grip. "They think the foster parents are clean, but they don't know. No one does."

The psychologist nodded, jotting down notes, his face unreadable.

Elizabeth continued, her voice growing distant as memories flooded in. "I've told you before—I know it was the foster parent. I've said it over and over, but... there's no record. Social Services says there's nothing."

The psychologist raised his brow. "No record? That's unusual. If you've reported it, there should be documentation. I'll look into it again, but for now, let's focus on your son."

He could see Elizabeth was unravelling, her anger a flimsy mask for her fear. She had lost control of her life once before, and the thought of it happening again—losing her children because of her past mistakes—was unbearable.

In the back of her mind, Elizabeth replayed her breakdown, the long, dark days spent in a hospital while her children were taken away. I can't go through that again. I can't lose them. She blinked back tears, trying to pull herself together, but the fear was suffocating.

The investigation into Tea Jay's injury was ongoing, and Elizabeth couldn't shake the feeling that all eyes were on her. Worse, she couldn't control the narrative. The nurse who had been on duty when Tea Jay was brought into the emergency room had since passed away, and the records had mysteriously been lost in a fire. The truth was buried under layers of uncertainty and suspicion.

Both Elizabeth and the foster parents were under investigation, each denying responsibility, each trapped in a web of unanswered questions. Elizabeth had witnesses—family members who could swear she wasn't there when Tea Jay was hurt—but Social Services was sceptical. They saw her past, her alcoholism, and her breakdown as reasons to doubt her. The weight of their suspicion pressed down on her, threatening to crush her.

She took a deep breath, her hands trembling. "They think I'm the one to blame. They'll always think it's me," she whispered, more to herself than to the psychologist.

"I understand that this is difficult, Mrs. M.," the psychologist said, his voice steady but firm. "But I need you to listen closely. Tea Jay... He's been through something traumatic, something that goes beyond his physical injuries. He'll struggle with emotional and psychological issues for the rest of his life. He might never learn to trust fully. He may find it difficult to form relationships. He'll likely feel abandoned, even if that's not the case. And this will shape him. It's already shaping him."

Elizabeth's breath hitched, her tears now falling freely. "Are you saying he's broken? My son... is broken?"

The psychologist hesitated before responding. "He's a very fragile child. With the right care, he can still grow and live a meaningful life. But... he'll need help. A lot of help. More than just physical treatment."

"I'm going to refer Tea Jay to a child psychiatrist. Dr. McClay. He's highly regarded in his field, and I believe he can help Tea Jay start healing—emotionally, at least."

The psychologist's words echoed in Elizabeth's mind, but all she could focus on was the overwhelming guilt, the looming investigation, and the suffocating fear of losing her children again. I've failed him.

Elizabeth starts drinking again, the pressure mounting with each passing day. In her mind, she is already the guilty party—her past always casts a long shadow. Social Services must see her as an easy target, someone to blame while the foster parents, with their clean records, escape unscathed.

"Just bleeding tell me! Why on earth won't my bloody son be the same again? C'mon, explain, Know-it-all! You think it's all my fault, don't ya?" Elizabeth screams at the psychologist.

"I understand you're upset, Mrs. M, but I can't tolerate this language. You need to calm down so I can explain, or I'll be forced to call the Police," the psychologist warns, his tone remaining professional.

He explains further, "Your son will struggle emotionally for his entire life. It's unlikely he will ever form healthy relationships or fully trust people. He may repress his feelings, and there will likely be emotional outbursts as he matures. He's unfortunately a very broken little boy."

Elizabeth's rage falters, replaced by despair. "Broken," she whispers, the word cutting deep.

A month after the psychologist's appointment, Tea Jay's older brother chooses to go out with friends instead of taking him to the lake as promised. That leaves Tea Jay alone with Uncle Rich, and fear begins to consume the boy.

Later that afternoon...

"Clean yourself up before we get up this bloody hill. Quick, fast, sharp. And don't open your mouth, or I'll get the ghost to kill ya," Rich snaps, his voice low and menacing.

Rich moves too quickly up the hill, leaving Tea Jay, only seven years old, alone and frightened, struggling to keep up. Lost and confused, Tea Jay finds himself wandering through Cooks Lane, unsure of how to get home. Tears stream down his face as fear grips his small heart.

As he tries to retrace his steps, an older boy steps into view—someone he recognizes but wishes he didn't.

The boy looms over Tea Jay, dressed in blue jeans and a white t-shirt with a Grim Reaper emblazoned on it. His eyes are dark and cold, and a scar stretches across his pale cheek.

"Please don't hurt me. I'll give you all my money," Tea Jay stammers, his hands trembling as he pulls out a few pennies.

The boy sneers. "Why are you shaking? You scared?"

"No... I've just got bad nerves. My hand's all burned," Tea Jay mutters, barely able to speak through the lump in his throat.

"Show me," the boy demands.

Tea Jay hesitates but lifts his hand. Before he can react, the bully shoves him into a nearby hedge filled with stinging nettles and spiders. The pain is instant and excruciating, as his skin burns and prickles all over. His screams shatter the quiet afternoon air, a desperate cry for help that no one answers at first.

A passerby, a man named Ron who knows Tea Jay's mother, hears the scream and rushes over. "You alright, lad?" he asks, concerned.

Tea Jay can't stop sobbing. He doesn't say a word, just nods and lets Ron help him out of the nettles.

"Let's get you home," Ron says gently, leading the boy back to his house.

Back at home, Elizabeth is furious. Tea Jay looks filthy, his clothes are wet, and he smells like dirt and sweat, and his face streaked with dry tears.

"Where the hell have you been, Tea Jay? And why are you wet? What's that smell?" she snaps angrily, her hands on her hips.

Before Tea Jay can answer, she turns on her brother. "Weren't you supposed to bring him home, Rich?"

"Ah, c'mon, sis. The kid's seven now. If he can't keep up, that's on him," Rich says, laughing.

Elizabeth scowls. "I'll ask you again, Tea Jay! Why are your trousers wet? What happened to you?"

"He probably fell in a puddle at the lake," Rich says, brushing it off.

Before Elizabeth can push further, Ron steps in, explaining how Tea Jay was attacked by a local bully. "He was shoved into stinging nettles. I think you should put some calamine lotion on the stings," Ron suggests.

The boy had pushed him into the stingers twice, laughing as TJ cried. It wasn't just the stings that hurt, but the way the boy made him feel—small and scared. TJ doesn't want to go outside anymore, worried he'll see the boy waiting to hurt him again and again.

Elizabeth's fury softens slightly as she listens to Ron, but she still looks at Tea Jay with exasperation.

That night, Tea Jay and his sister Lacey share their mother's bed. Tea Jay still can't sleep alone ever since the ghost incident, so their mother lets them stay in her room.

A week later, Lacey wakes up in the middle of the night to find Tea Jay on the floor, playing with their mother's cigarette lighter.

"Ah, I'm telling mommy, Tea Jay," Lacey says, her voice full of fear.

Tea Jay, unaware of the danger, just shrugs. "It's okay. I'm just playing," he says, continuing to flick the lighter.

Lacey begs him to stop, but he doesn't listen. Before they know it, the stuffing underneath the bed catches fire.

Within moments, the entire room is ablaze. Lacey screams for their mother. "Mommy, Mommy! Wake up! Tea Jay set the house on fire!"

Smoke billows from beneath the bedroom door, filling the air with thick, choking fumes. Elizabeth, disoriented from sleep and the alcohol from the night before, yells for her brother.

"Rich! Get up, you drunken bastard! That little pissant's trying to kill us all! He's set the house on fire! Call the fire brigade, quick!"

In her fury, she lashes out at Tea Jay, slapping him so hard he nearly falls down the stairs. If not for Uncle Rich, the child might have tumbled to his death.

"Little bastard!" Rich snarls as he slaps Tea Jay again, this time across the face, sending him reeling backward.

Despite the chaos, Rich manages to get everyone out of the house just as the fire consumes more of the structure. Tea Jay suffers a burn on his knee, but otherwise, they all make it out unharmed.

As fire engines pull up to the scene, the house is an inferno. Windows shatter, and black smoke pours from the roof. Neighbours gather on the green, watching in horror.

"I heard Tea Jay set fire to the house because he saw a ghost," one neighbour whispers.

Elizabeth is still fuming. In her drunken state, she slaps Tea Jay again, and the neighbours mutter among themselves, encouraging her to punish the boy further.

"I need a bloody drink," Elizabeth mutters to her neighbour, April, as she stumbles away from Tea Jay.

She raises her hand to strike him once more, but a fireman intervenes, stopping her. "That's enough! He's just a child. He didn't mean to set fire to your home," the fireman says sternly. "How did he get the matches?"

"They're my children! Don't tell me how to raise them! He must've gotten my lighter from my bag. Look what the little bastard's done to my house!" Elizabeth shouts back.

The fireman sees Tea Jay's frightened, tear-streaked face and decides to take him into the fire engine, away from the chaos. He removes his helmet and speaks gently to the boy.

"Where did you get the lighter, son?" the fireman asks softly.

"I found it by the bed," Tea Jay whispers.

"Did you take it from your mother's bag? Tell me the truth now," the fireman says, his voice firm but kind.

Tea Jay hesitates before answering, "No, it was on the bed. I didn't mean to set fire to mommy's house."

The fireman sighs, his heart heavy. "Poor child. The mother probably left the lighter out in plain view. I'll have to put that in my report," he thinks to himself.

But no report is ever submitted. Instead, Social Services suggests that Tea Jay stay with his natural father while the situation is investigated. His mother doesn't want Tea Jay near her or the other children.

For the third time in his short life, Tea Jay feels utterly abandoned by his mother. He desperately wishes for people to understand that the fire was an accident, but the weight of rejection and blame is too much to bear.

In just three years—half his life—Tea Jay has known nothing but rejection, abuse, and pain. His heart has been torn apart by the people who were supposed to protect him.

Now, as he stays with his father, Tea Jay yearns for love and acceptance. He wants to understand why he feels so unloved, why everything seems to go wrong, and why the pain never ends.

For the rest of his life, these deep emotional wounds will follow him, shaping his relationships, his sense of self-worth, and his ability to trust others. His journey through life will be marked by the scars of his past, both visible and invisible.

An argument between Elizabeth and her neighbour escalated quickly after her neighbour hammers against the front door. Jay watched from the window, his heart pounding as insults flew back and forth. His mother, Elizabeth, stood face-to-face with the neighbour, her fists clenched as they hurled curses at one another.

"You're a bloody menace! Your boy nearly blinded my son!" the neighbour shouted, pointing an accusatory finger toward the house.

Elizabeth didn't back down. "Your son started it! You should control him before throwing stones in glass houses!"

Jay cringed as he saw the neighbour's son, clutching his bleeding face, glaring up at the window where he was hiding. The memory of the brick he had thrown that afternoon flashed in Jay's mind, and a wave of guilt washed over him. He hadn't meant to cause so much damage.

Suddenly, things turned physical. Elizabeth shoved the neighbour, who yanked at Elizabeth's hair in return. A tangle of arms and shouts broke out, and Jay could hardly believe what he was seeing. His mother screamed, "Get off me, you witch!" as she pushed the woman away.

The neighbour's, seething with fury, stumbled back. Without hesitation, she grabbed a brick lying nearby and threw it toward the house. The sound of shattering glass pierced the air as the front window cracked open, shards scattering everywhere.

"That'll teach you!" the neighbour spat before storming off, pulling her son behind her.

Elizabeth stood frozen for a moment, breathing heavily, her eyes darting between the broken window and her boys inside. Jay could feel the tension in the air thickening, but neither of them said a word.

There was an eerie silence after the neighbour disappeared, and for a second, everything felt unnervingly still.

Jay turned to his mother, expecting her to shout or scream, but all she did was mutter to herself, pacing around the room, rubbing her temples. "Where's Trixie?" she asked suddenly, looking toward the back door.

"She must've got out during all the commotion. She'll be back," Elizabeth said absentmindedly, still focused on the shattered window.

But deep down, Jay had a sinking feeling in his stomach. He hadn't seen Trixie since the fight started.

Hours passed, and night had fallen. Suddenly, a loud knock at the door jolted them all. The sound startled Elizabeth, and Jay's heart skipped a beat.

The knock came again, harder this time. Elizabeth glanced toward the window, then at her sons, her expression clouded with concern. "Stay here," she ordered, her voice barely steady as she moved toward the door.

Jay's pulse quickened. "It's the police," he whispered to his brother. "They've come because of what I did. They're here because of me."

Another knock, even more insistent, echoed through the room. Elizabeth hesitated at the door, her hand shaking as she reached for the lock.

With trembling fingers, she opened the door.

Two police officers stood on the doorstep; their faces unreadable. Elizabeth's gaze shifted between them, her breath catching as her eyes fell on one of the officers. He was holding something.

Her heart pounded in her chest. What is that? Handcuffs? Papers? Something else?

The object gleamed faintly under the dim porch light, casting an ominous glow. Her mind raced, thinking of all the possible reasons they were there. The neighbour must have called them about the fight, or maybe Jay's brick had caused more trouble than she'd thought.

But there was something off about the way the officer held the object. Elizabeth squinted, her vision focusing on the item in his hand. It was round, metallic...

The weight in her chest grew heavier. Her eyes widened.

The knock at the door suddenly seemed far more ominous than before.

HOME FROM HOME

Tea Jay feels all alone, afraid and unloved. In his young, abused heart, he yearns for someone to love, accept, and take care of him. His tummy always seems to tumble as he constantly feels the fire of his tears within. He constantly has the same reoccurring nightmare of the man in his room and begins to experience anger and bitterness, uncontrollable emotions far too early in his life.

He often says to himself,

"Why doesn't my mom love me? And why did she tell the fireman a lie about how I got her lighter?"

Tea Jay doesn't understand the harsh realities of life, nor the consequences that certain truths may bring.

TJ has been taken to an unfamiliar place that feels alien to him, a home belonging to a man who says he is his father. But to TJ, this man is nothing more than a stranger, never present in his life. Michael, standing about five foot seven with a large frame, only has one eye, the other lost in a childhood accident involving a bow and arrow. His brown hair is combed over to hide thinning patches, and his complexion is perpetually flushed. He's always dressed smartly, favouring white or blue shirts with polished leather slip-ons, as if trying to maintain appearances. Michael's home—a four-bedroom council house in the suburbs of Birmingham—feels as foreign to TJ as the man who owns it. Despite the physical space, there's an emotional distance between father and son that's far greater.

As you walk through the front door, the aroma of roast dinner greets you. A short hallway, about ten feet long, leads into the kitchen. Brown ceramic tiles cover the floors in the hallway, kitchen, and living room. Facing the kitchen windows, you'll see a double sink that looks out onto the back garden. A heavy wooden breakfast bar, built by Tea Jay's father, stands to the left, between the back door and the main window.

The dining room, to the left, holds a big pine table with six chairs. To the left of the dining room, the open-plan living room holds a black leather three-seater sofa against one wall and a matching single-seater in the far corner, where Michael watches country & western films on Sundays. The magnolia-coloured walls of both the living room and kitchen display a few pictures of stock-car races.

In the front garden sits a white Vauxhall Viva in pieces—a never-ending project for Michael.

Tea Jay thinks to himself,

"This isn't my dad; I don't know him. A dad is someone who plays with me and takes me to the park."

Tea Jay and his siblings have endured psychological abuse from both parents, neither of whom were emotionally present. While putting food on the table and providing a roof over their heads, his parents failed to give their children the emotional guidance and love they needed during their most vulnerable and formative years.

Amidst his tears and mood swings, Tea Jay wonders,

"I don't remember who my daddy is."

Fear consumes him. He doesn't understand what's happening to him, and his mind is too young to process his emotions. As far back as he can remember, he's known nothing but fear, smacks, and hiding under the bed with his sister to escape the loud voices and terror.

Since before the fire that left him scarred, Tea Jay's sense of security was ripped away, leaving him feeling unloved and unworthy. His fear is deep-rooted—so profound that nothing or no one can seem to reach it.

His little hands tremble for many reasons, including:

1. The psychological trauma caused by the abuse, both physical and emotional.

2. The physical damage from the third-degree burns on his hand, and the constant reminder of the fire, which haunts him even more than the pain.

The only person Tea Jay trusts is his Uncle Rob, but even he only visits every other Sunday to have a pint with his brother.

Tea Jay remains frightened of most people, unsure who might hurt him next. He's developing severe trust issues, especially for a child his age.

His half-brothers and sisters are initially confused as to why Tea Jay calls their father "dad," since they've never met him. At first, they push him away, but over time, they begin to accept him. Still, Tea Jay keeps them at a distance, craving trust but too lost in his fear to accept it.

Within months, Tea Jay is sent to a new school in another part of the Midlands. He struggles to adjust as the local children hear about the fire. They begin bullying him, throwing cruel insults like "Swan Vesta" and calling him a firebug. The taunting never stops.

"You're the murderer who tried to kill his family, aren't you, firebug?"

Tea Jay comes home from school, terrified and crying, to find Sarah, his social worker, and his mother in the living room.

"Why are you crying, Tea Jay?" Sarah asks gently.

"Someone at school said I tried to kill mom and Lacey with the fire," Tea Jay blurts out.

His mother breaks down, sobbing uncontrollably.

"I can't do this! It isn't fair to my son! Come here, my darling," she says softly, holding out her arms.

But Tea Jay's face is filled with fear and sadness. His expression is closed off, his gaze fixed on the floor as he clasps his little hands together. He refuses to go to his mother, bowing his head in silent pain.

"Tea Jay, aren't you glad to see mommy?" Sarah says, trying to encourage him.

Slowly, Tea Jay walks nervously toward his mother, his head still bowed, eyes fixed on the ground. He desperately wants to be liked, loved, and accepted, but fear holds him back. He hesitates, unsure whether it's safe to throw his little arms around her. In his heart, he believes she might hit him.

"Tea Jay, we're going to see someone today who can help you," Sarah says as Tea Jay sits on his mother's lap, resting his head against her chest.

"This place we're going to is very close to Nannie's, Tea Jay," his mother adds softly, hoping to reassure him.

"Why don't you love me, Mom? Have I done something wrong?" Tea Jay whispers, his small voice thick with emotion as he wipes his tears away.

"Of course, Mommy loves you! You're just very poorly, and Mommy wants to make you all better. Do you understand?" his mother replies, her voice trembling with emotion.

"Can I come home, please, Mom?" Tea Jay asks, his face etched with sadness.

"Yes, you can, soon enough. I promise," Elizabeth says, tears glistening in her eyes.

The social worker exchanges a glance with Elizabeth before turning to Tea Jay. "Come on then, Tea Jay, off we go," she says gently.

Tea Jay is taken to a place called Charles Burns Clinic.

Charles Burns is a psychiatric clinic specializing in the diagnosis and treatment of children's mental health. The building resembles a sprawling college complex, nestled within the serene surroundings of Kings Heath Park. The long drive leading to the clinic is lined with tall trees, their branches forming a tunnel as they descend a steep hill. On the right, the trees appear to grow taller, while on the left, they seem to sink into a vast forest that stretches far beyond view.

"Come on, Tea Jay, we're here," Sarah says softly.

For a moment, as they arrive, Elizabeth dozes off in the car, only to be jarred awake by a nightmare. She suddenly cries out, "It's not his fault—leave him alone!"

Startled, Sarah looks at her, confused. "What do you mean, Elizabeth? What's not his fault?"

Elizabeth, wide-eyed and shaken, quickly brushes it off. "Nothing... I just fell asleep for a second," she mutters, her expression revealing fear.

Despite an investigation into the fire, the full story behind why Tea Jay started the blaze was never truly uncovered. The question remains unspoken, buried beneath layers of guilt and denial.

Inside the clinic, Tea Jay is taken to a room filled with toys and children his age. A two-way mirror allows staff to observe the interactions. But Tea Jay refuses to engage. He shies away from the other children, retreating to a corner, overwhelmed with the fear of rejection. His small frame trembles, his stomach churning, as he fights back the tears that relentlessly threaten to surface.

Through the two-way mirror, Elizabeth watches him, her face streaked with tears. Her anguish is palpable, as if she's trapped in her own emotional prison. The psychiatrist places a gentle hand on her shoulder, but Elizabeth remains lost in her thoughts.

What am I going to do? she wonders. If I admit I left the lighter and cigarettes out, they'll take all my kids for good. The weight of her guilt presses down, suffocating her.

"Elizabeth," the psychiatrist calls out, noticing her patient lost in thought. "Are you okay?"

Elizabeth doesn't respond, her gaze fixed on Tea Jay through the mirror.

Later, as Tea Jay is brought out of the room, Elizabeth kneels before him, her voice trembling as she says, "Tea Jay, you have to stay here for a little while longer. Then you can come home. I promise."

"Mom, you said I could come home! You lied again! I don't like it here. Why can't I come home?" Tea Jay sobs, his voice rising in anger. "I don't love you anymore! Leave me alone! I never want to see you again!"

A year passes, and though Tea Jay settles into Charles Burns, his behaviour becomes erratic. Mood swings and outbursts become frequent. One day, a nurse spots him sneaking out of a shop with another boy, a box of matches clutched in their hands. Both boys are marched back to the clinic, and Tea Jay is sent straight to bed, punishment looming over him.

Months later, another visit from his mother, Uncle Rob, and Nanny Louise is arranged. But when the nurse tells him the news, Tea Jay retreats, hiding behind her, unwilling to face his mother.

"I don't love you anymore! Leave me alone!" he shouts, before fleeing into the nearby woods, tears streaming down his cheeks. He refuses to return until he's sure his mother has gone.

The emotional toll on Tea Jay is immense. His world becomes a tangled web of confusion, mistrust, and distorted realities. He grows attached to one of the nurses, Dawn—a kind, caring woman who offers him the warmth and affection he craves.

Dawn is petite, with ocean-blue eyes and long, wavy brown hair. She has a soft smile and an approachable demeanor. Tea Jay becomes fiercely attached to her, often growing jealous when she spends time with other children. His affection becomes possessive, but he can't understand that Dawn is not his alone.

By Christmas 1979, two years into his stay at Charles Burns, Tea Jay's nightmares of the man in his room and flashbacks of the fire still haunt him. After three successful visits from his mother, there's talk of him going home for the holiday. However, when the psychiatric team assesses him, they decide it's too risky.

One day, a different nurse, Bernadette, approaches him. She leads him into the office, where his psychiatrist, Dr. McClay, waits. Tea Jay sits down, his heart pounding.

"Tea Jay," Dr. McClay says with a heavy tone. "I've got some very bad news about your nurse, Dawn. She can't be your nurse anymore."

"Tea Jay, do you know what dying & heaven means?" the psychiatrist asks.

"Did she die because of me?" Tea Jay cries out.

"No, she didn't die because of you, Tea Jay," Bernadette says while she cuddles the little boy.

"Anyway, Tea Jay, this is Bernadette, she's going to be looking after you from now on. Are you okay?" the psychiatrist asks.

Bernadette's very good-looking, and she has the pleasant scent of Yves Saint Lauren around her. She has about the same build as Dawn had and wears very similar clothes. She has piercing hazel eyes and quite a petite figure. Tea Jay takes to his new nurse almost immediately.

A week later, one of the male nurses asks Tea Jay if he'd like to play with some other children on the scramble-net. However, as Tea Jay reaches the top of the net, the same male nurse who asks him if he'd like to play jumps onto the net. Tea Jay's accidently catapulted off the climbing frame, head first. He smashes his head against the concrete, and the force of it knocks him unconscious for a few minutes. Upon examination, one of the psychiatrists suggests a trip to the hospital. It was found that although stitches were needed and there would be a nasty bump to the left-hand side of his forehead, there was no permanent damage.

Nevertheless, Tea Jay's mother is furious and complains, seeking legal advice against the home.

It's now Christmas 1980. Tea Jay is ten years old and has been in Charles Burns for nearly three years. He's been told he's progressing marvellously, and there's every chance he might be able to visit home. He's been allowed to have short day visits to his nanny Lou and one or two shopping visits with his mother. However, he's not been allowed to stay away overnight. Tea Jay gets all excited and tells Bernadette, whom he's become very fond of and attached to.

As Tea Jay plays outside a week after he's allowed his overnight visit, he notices his psychiatrist in his office through one of the windows. He calls to the psychiatrist.

"Can I go back home, Dr McClay?"

The doctor writes on a large piece of paper:

"MAYBE, BUT NOT AT THE MOMENT."

Dr McClay is a very pleasant, slim gentleman from Glasgow. He has bushy grey eyebrows and a bald head. He's about five feet eight and very smartly dressed, maybe in his mid-sixties. He loves to play golf with one or two of the other doctors at the clinic.

A month or two later, Tea Jay sees Dr McClay again through the window. He shouts the question, asking if he can go home. This goes on for a few more months until Dr McClay suddenly notices that the boy seems to have given up asking the same question he had been for a while.

He calls out to him in his deep Scottish accent.

"Are you alright, Tea Jay?"

When Tea Jay nods to indicate he is okay, the psychiatrist asks him, "Aren't you going to ask me the same question you've been making a fuss about for months, Tea Jay?"

Tea Jay looks confused, then all of a sudden, he realises what the psychiatrist is on about and gives Dr McClay a deeply troubled look.

"Well, Tea Jay, ask me the same question you've been asking for the past few months," the psychiatrist insists with a smile.

"Can I go home?" Tea Jay shouts.

"YES!" Dr McClay writes on a piece of flipchart paper.

Tea Jay's tummy tumbles and pushes a flood of tears to the surface when it's time for him to go home and say goodbye to his favourite nurse, Bernadette.

"I want you to be my mom; I don't want to go home," Tea Jay cries out to Bernadette while they both pack the rest of his belongings into his little suitcase.

"Tea Jay, you have a mother who loves you very much. I've explained that I'm only your nurse, and we agreed that one day you would go back home, and I'd no longer be your nurse. Do you remember?" Bernadette says to the frightened little boy.

"I don't want to go home. I'm scared!" Tea Jay cries out.

"There's nothing to be scared of. Come on, you're going on holiday tomorrow, and you're starting a new school called Bennetts Well in a couple of weeks. You're going home today to your family, who love you very much," Bernadette finally says.

Tea Jay gets all excited because he's going to Devon Cliffs for a week's holiday with Gingerbread, a one-parent group his mother's been attending every Monday night with Lacey and Jay.

Tea Jay has never been away on holiday before, and he suddenly feels something different and strange. He starts to experience peace that he's never felt. He suddenly starts to feel a strange, unfamiliar sensation of what he imagines to be liked, loved, and accepted by his mom and family. However, although Tea Jay enjoys the holiday and has loads of fun, the reality soon hits home as he starts his new school.

Tea Jay has changed an awful lot over the past few years. He's definitely not the same little boy he once was.

"Mom, can I have an apple?" Tea Jay asks.

"Tea Jay, why do you keep asking permission for things like fruit, milk, and biscuits? I've told you before, this is your home. You don't need to ask permission for anything. You're allowed to help yourself, okay?" his mother says.

Tea Jay's mother doesn't quite understand that every family member he once felt close to is more or less a stranger to him. The once-strong sibling and motherly connection he felt seems to have been lost. He feels very much alone and won't show any affection to Lacey, Jason, or his mother. Any emotional connection he once felt seems to have been permanently broken.

One morning, a few months on, Tea Jay starts to experience frightening memories and continually ducks as he enters his house when his mother answers the door.

"Why are Tea Jay's hands shaking, and why does he keep ducking when he walks past you when you let him in, mom?" Lacey asks.

"You know why, Lacey; stop asking stupid questions. Do you pissing-well hear me?" her mom snaps.

One day, Tea Jay finds his uncle Rich in his mom's dress and tights.

Immediate fear grips him as he has a sudden flashback of the night he saw the ghost and the day his uncle Rich took him fishing. Suddenly coming to his senses, although he goes ice-cold, he darts back upstairs into his mother's room. His whole body shakes in terror, ice-cold, and in floods of tears, he finds her face down on the bed, still half-drunk from the night before and half asleep.

"What's wrong? What's wrong? Why've you fuckin' woke me up, Tea?" his mother screams.

Unable to contain secrets any longer, Tea Jay finally breaks down and attempts to tell his mother what's been going on.

Still half-asleep, his mother can't take anything in. Alcohol, being her master, controls her thoughts and clouds her judgement.

"Leave me alone. I'll talk to him later," his mother shouts at Tea Jay.

Tea Jay's nightmares and flashbacks of seeing a man in his room are becoming more frequent. He is haunted by fear, convinced his uncle Rich knows what has been happening. The isolation worsens, and he spends most of his time crying for reasons he can't explain, hiding under his bed, the safest place he can find.

A month passes, and Tea Jay finally returns from Charles Burns. He manages to settle into his junior school, though he finds himself in a year below Jay. He's not entirely comfortable with it, but it's where his new friends are, so he adjusts. Academically, however, he struggles, having been out of mainstream school for nearly three years.

It doesn't take long for the school to notice. Tea Jay's learning is far behind his classmates. Eventually, they decide the best course of action is to move him down another year to help him catch up. This decision makes sense in light of his age and academic level, but for Tea Jay, it feels like punishment for something beyond his control.

In the background, whispers and laughs follow him wherever he goes. One boy, Grey, takes particular pleasure in mocking him.

"Don't upset him, he'll burn your house down like he did his own!" Grey taunts from the back of the classroom, drawing snickers from others.

Tea Jay tries to stay composed but feels the fire building inside him. "I didn't burn my house down, it was an accident!" he yells, his voice breaking with frustration.

Grey laughs louder, his words cutting deep. "Then why were you in the loony bin? Huh? Murderer!"

"Shut up, ginger nut!" Tea Jay snaps back, anger boiling to the surface.

"Wait 'til after school, murderer. We'll see who's laughing then." Grey sneers, just as the teacher walks back into the room.

She notices the tension instantly, barking at Grey. "That's enough! One more word from you, and you'll be staying after class."

Grey backs down, but Tea Jay can't hold back the tears. The shame, the ridicule, it all feels too much.

"Come on, Tea Jay, no need for tears. Haven't you heard that old saying? 'Sticks and stones may break my bones, but words will never hurt me.'" The teacher tries to reassure him, though the words fall flat.

Tea Jay doesn't understand. "Why do they hurt so much then?" he mutters, more to himself than to her.

"Fists hurt, too!" Grey interjects, earning himself a swift smack on the back of the head from the teacher.

"Grey, Tea Jay, you're both staying behind," she declares, her patience worn thin.

After the classroom empties, the teacher addresses Grey first, reprimanding him for bullying. She explains to both boys that Tea Jay has been through enough already and doesn't need additional torment. She forces them to shake hands and insists they try to get along. The moment is hollow, but the boys comply before heading off to their next class.

Even after this confrontation, Tea Jay continues to struggle. He feels like an outsider—too old for his year group but too far behind academically to move forward. He begins to act out, seeking attention in the only ways he knows how. He arrives at school in 18-hole Doc Martens and skin-tight jeans, his head freshly shaven by his neighbours. His rebellious streak intensifies, and he's often sent home for his behaviour.

Then, one day, while watching TV, Tea Jay hears a loud commotion outside.

"Put the money through the letterbox, you dirty bastard runt, and piss off!" His mother's voice echoes through the house as she shouts at his uncle. "You're not welcome here anymore, you dirty bastard! I'll have the coppers on you!"

It's Christmas 1982. Although Tea Jay has a few friends, he still feels out of place, like a square peg in a round hole. His mother wants to move—they've been burgled recently, and she can't stand the house anymore, with all its bad memories. She's already applied for a council exchange.

By Christmas 1984, Tea Jay and his family have moved a few miles away. His brother Jay is getting into worse trouble, involved with bad company, in and out of remand centres, smoking weed, sniffing glue, and committing burglaries.

Despite all this, Tea Jay's family attends a one-parent support group called Gingerbread, where they meet other single-parent families. Jay quickly gains a bad reputation for his behaviour, and Tea Jay is caught in the fallout.

Tea Jay, meanwhile, has become deeply involved in the Mod scene. He idolizes the film Quadrophenia and forms a friendship with another boy from Gingerbread who shares his interests. His new friend attends a different school, and Tea Jay becomes obsessed with transferring there. After relentless begging, his mother finally gives in and agrees to the change, hoping it will make him happy.

But shortly after transferring schools, disaster strikes. Jay is accused of burglarizing Tea Jay's friend's house. Tea Jay is terrified that his new friend will believe he was involved. Desperate, he begs his mother to transfer him back to his old school, but this time she stands firm.

"Deal with it," she says coldly.

His fears are soon confirmed—his friend turns into his worst enemy, and Tea Jay begins to regret the decision to switch schools in the first place. He starts skipping class regularly, getting warnings from the school that if his attendance doesn't improve, there will be serious consequences. To escape the pain, Tea Jay turns to drugs—smoking cannabis and sniffing gas to drown out his fearful thoughts.

Finally, Tea Jay learns that his friend's family has discovered someone else was responsible for the burglary. It wasn't Jay after all. But the damage has already been done, and Tea Jay is left in a state of isolation, the few bonds he had built now shattered.

However, Tea Jay becomes convinced that everyone is out to get him.

At his mother's request, social services intervene. His unruly behaviour—smoking drugs, being abusive, and sleeping in his clothes—has escalated. But beneath it all, Tea Jay still longs for the love and acceptance of his friends and family.

Each morning, he attends school just long enough to register before sneaking off. He believes he's too clever to get caught, but the authorities and his social worker are quickly on his trail. With his mother's agreement, Tea Jay is sent to an Assessment Centre in Solihull, designed to monitor his behaviour and educational needs.

The centre itself is small, housing only around twelve boys and girls. Nestled in a quiet Birmingham suburb, it looks more like a small school than a children's home. Inside, the walls are plain and unremarkable, the floors covered in industrial brown carpet. The common areas offer modest comforts: a pool table, a dining area, and a TV room tucked in the corner. Tea Jay's room, decorated with superhero posters, overlooks a field. His small world has now become even more confined.

The first person he meets is his key worker, Nita, a young woman in her twenties with a warm demeaner. She's tall and slim, with a kind smile and a soothing presence. To Tea Jay, she's a beacon of stability in his chaotic world.

Six weeks pass, and Tea Jay starts to form a strong attachment to Nita. He looks forward to their one-on-one sessions, mistaking her professional kindness for something more personal. As the lines blur in his mind, he tries to push the boundaries.

"Nita, do you have a boyfriend?" he asks one day, his heart pounding.

She laughs, deflecting the question. "Why, you trying to chat me up, Tea Jay?" she teases.

"I love you," Tea Jay blurts out, his cheeks burning.

Nita shakes her head gently, a mix of amusement and discomfort in her eyes. "I'm flattered, but I'm your key worker. I'm here to help you, not date you."

Tea Jay doesn't fully understand her response. He's not used to affection, especially not the kind Nita gives, and he confuses her attention with love. Soon, his feelings become an obsession, and he withdraws from everything else.

The managers decide it's best for Tea Jay to be assigned a male care worker. The shift leaves him feeling rejected, abandoned once again. His personal hygiene deteriorates, and he isolates himself even further, refusing to bathe or change his clothes.

Tea Jay grows increasingly defiant. He refuses to leave the centre, convinced the kids from his brother's burglary are waiting outside to hurt him. In a moment of rebellion, he lights a spliff right in front of a care worker and a police officer. It doesn't take long for the authorities to take him into custody.

As Tea Jay faces juvenile court, his mother, social worker, and Nita sit with him in a meeting room filled with grim-faced adults. The head of care asks him why he believes everyone is against him, but Tea Jay can't give an answer. His fear of retribution keeps him silent, his mind locked in survival mode.

After a lengthy discussion, it is decided that Tea Jay will be moved to a children's home outside of Solihull until he finishes school. His mother, overwhelmed, breaks down in tears.

"I told you this would happen if you kept wagging school!" she cries, her voice trembling.

Two weeks later, Tea Jay meets Wayne, a social worker from a rural children's home. Wayne is older, his heavy northern accent accompanied by the thick smell of cigars.

"Hello, Tea Jay," Wayne says, offering a hand. "I'm from Colington Court."

Tea Jay pulls a face as the stench of tobacco hits him. "Is that cigar choking you, young man? Sorry, La," Wayne chuckles.

Colington Court is far from Birmingham, a sprawling mansion deep in the countryside. The imposing building is surrounded by acres of woodland, the long driveway snaking through trees that seem to close in like shadows. The place feels haunted to Tea Jay, its sheer size and eerie stillness only adding to his sense of isolation. It houses some fifty boys and girls, aged six to eighteen. There are acres of land and woodland surrounding the two-mile driveway from the main road up to the main building.

A week later, after an outburst at the assessment centre, Tea Jay is forcibly taken to Colington Court, with his brother and one of his closest friends from the assessment centre allowed to accompany him for the journey. As they arrive, Tea Jay stares at the building, dread tightening in his chest. This was his new home, and the only question that lingered in his mind was—would he ever escape the darkness that seemed to follow him wherever he went?

It has a reception opposite four terrapin blocks that act as an education centre. There's a games room for the children to play in at the rear. There's also a converted barn that's been made into another education block as well as staff accommodation a few hundred yards from the main building. The main mansion looks out over many miles of scenic beautiful countryside.

It's now June 1985, and Tea Jay's approaching his fifteenth birthday. He feels lost, depressed, and absolutely broken. He's not only amongst other children he doesn't know, but he feels frightened because he's hundreds of miles from home in the country.

Tea Jay waves goodbye to his brother and his friend as his social worker takes them back home to the Wood, a place Tea Jay never thought he'd miss so much as he does right now.

As Tea Jay looks out into the vast distance of miles of rolling hills and scenery that stretches on for miles, his mind yearns for something or someone familiar. His stomach tumbles, and tears start to surface. The memory of Charles Burns suddenly returns, and a canyon of tears soak his red face as he cries uncontrollably while sitting on a wall, looking out into the countryside. In his heart, all he really wants is a glimmer of home in the distance. Yet, in reality, he knows he's fooling himself. One of the other lads from the home comes over to comfort him.

"It's okay, you're allowed to cry; it's good for you. What's your name?" says a cockney lad.

"Fuck off, leave me alone," Tea Jay snaps.

"There's no need to be like that; I'm only trying to be friendly," the boy replies.

A Welsh kid approaches Tea Jay and asks why he's crying. Taff, as everyone calls him, explains how everyone at the home is in the same boat. He asks Tea Jay why he's there.

"Because I was being bullied and wouldn't go to school," Tea Jay says.

"I'm here because I was caught stealing cars, and my parents are gone. At least you've got a family," Taff laughs.

"Come on, I'll introduce you around," Taff says.

Later that evening, a staff member named Dave calls Tea Jay.

"Come for a smoke, Tea Jay. I'm your key-worker, by the way," Dave says.

"I'm allowed to smoke? But I'm only fourteen," Tea Jay replies.

"Yes, you're allowed four a day, mainly after meals. There are three house groups here. You're in the intermediates, which means we have control of your cigarettes and money. There are juniors for the younger ones and seniors for those older than fifteen. But mind you, if you misbehave, there are consequences. Now, I've noticed you swear a lot, so you'll stay in the intermediates until we see improvement," Dave explains.

Tea Jay is taken to the boot-room, where the other kids and staff smoke. The boot-room houses the work boots for the older children allowed out for work experience.

For the first few months, Tea Jay struggles to adjust to his new surroundings. However, he eventually makes new friends. Apart from making friends, he finds out he's allowed £4 a week pocket money and discovers he's already got a substantial amount saved in the office. He's also given a clothing grant worth over £400.

Tea Jay suddenly feels in his element, wearing stylish clothes and feeling good about himself because of his appearance. He believes everyone will finally accept him because he's dressed well. Yet behind the material things, Tea Jay remains sad and broken, craving love and acceptance from those closest to him.

After a few months, Tea Jay is finally allowed home for a visit the day before his fifteenth birthday.

On the day of his home visit, one of the locals calls out to him.

"I'm after you! Your brother robbed my house! Since he's locked up, I'll take it out on you!"

Tea Jay climbs on his mother's porch roof to avoid the bully. Just as the boy tries to climb up after him, Tea Jay's mother, Elizabeth, approaches.

"Eh, leave my pissing Babbie alone or I'll pissing brain ya. "Tea Jay's mother shouts.

The bully shouts a lode of abuse then walks off quickly.

"Why was he shouting at you, Tea Jay? It looked like he was about to give you a good pasting. What's going on, need I ask?" Tea Jay's mother shouts at Tea Jay.

"I'll give you three guesses, mom," Tea Jay whimpers under his breath.

"Jay again! Even when he's in prison, he's still causing bloody trouble and bringing our family name down," his mother says.

"This is why I didn't go to school in the first place because if they can't get to Jay, they go for his family," Tea Jay says.

"Well, I'm not going out; I'm staying in," Tea Jay says.

"You can't hide forever; you've done nothing wrong, Tea Jay."

"Try telling them that, mom! Do you really believe they're going to listen? Come on, mom, really, this is Chelmsley Wood after all," Tea Jay says sarcastically.

"You can't keep running, Tea Jay!"

Every time there's an incident where there's a threat of violence or someone approaches Tea Jay in an aggressive manner, he always closes up and freezes. His stomach tumbles in utter fear at the sight of any animosity. This is primarily because there's a sudden and profound psychological reminder of what happened many years earlier when his hand was forcibly held under boiling hot water.

Unfortunately, since he was scalded, both of Tea Jay's hands have always had a violent tremor. An awful lot of kids Tea Jay's age tend to bully and pick on him because they automatically assume that it's nothing but cowardly fear as to why he's shaking. The fact that he's suffering from the physical and psychological abuse of third-degree burns doesn't cross the minds of the local bullies. A lot of people would rather snarl and make unnecessary, unfair assumptions.

After about ten to twelve months, Tea Jay has no choice but to try and settle into his new surroundings. Nevertheless, after a while, Tea Jay realises that there's an awful lot of abuse occurring at the home. However, he's frightened of complaining because although he knows categorically that the abuse is definitely occurring, he believes in his heart and gets the all too familiar ache in his chest that spells hope-lessness and believes no one will believe him. This is because he has the impression his social worker will side with the establishment and agree that Tea Jay's just a problem child and therefore attention-seeking.

Tea Jay writes a letter to his mother complaining that there's bul-lying occurring at the children's home. He explains to his mother that if he or any of the other children misbehave, they're thrown into the Sin-Bin, which is a locked tiny room for hours on end.

In one incident, two of the Key Workers made Tea Jay and a couple of kids about Tea Jay's age lie on their backs on the floor in the office. They were made to lift up their legs while they were physically abused several times with "Rats-Tales," made from a wet tea towel that they would pop, flicking the wet towel on their legs and backsides. It would really sting and come very sharp.

One of the care managers belittles one of the kids who misbehaves and threatens to send them back to the detention centre where they came from.

"These are nothing but public nuisances and problem children; who's going to believe them and not us if they complain?" the care manager thinks to himself.

The very same care manager walks past Tea Jay and deliberately pushes him full-force onto the hard floor.

The care manager's name is Dick. He's over six feet tall and very muscular, into his rugby. There's absolutely no match to a four-teen-year-old minor. He's got dark, quite sinister eyes and finds it amusing to see a child helpless on the floor.

"Out of sight, out of mind, I guess," runs through Tea Jay's head as he looks Dick's way.

"Did you just say something, Tea Jay?" Dick asks as he pushes Tea Jay over yet again.

"Nothing!" Tea Jay replies with an angry stare.

On the football pitch, the same manager deliberately takes your legs from beneath you or just pushes you over as he runs after the ball.

Tea Jay speaks to his mom on the phone in the office because she's read his letter, which she received last week. She's obviously concerned, so she's not only complained to Tea Jay's social worker but directly to the children's home as well. The same home manager whom Tea Jay complained about and another member of staff are in the office and assure Tea Jay's mother that nothing untoward was happening at the home. They challenge Tea Jay while his mother is on the phone, asking why he'd made up such nonsense and exaggerating the truth. They explain to Tea Jay that in football, people can get rough and assure his mother that he's being properly taken care of while in the establishment.

The home also explains to his mother that they've never had any complaints like this before. Even though Tea Jay's mother lets it go on this one occasion, she still rips into them on the phone, threatening to go to the police.

She informs the home that she intends to keep her son's letter just in case she needs to use it as evidence in the future.

After the incident on the phone, the manager tells Tea Jay that he won't be going home this weekend and makes him sit in the Sin-Bin for hours. He tells Tea Jay that he's just a troublemaker, and if he wants to tell tales and run to his mother every time there's an issue, he can pay the price.

One Monday morning, Tea Jay and another kid about his own age decide to run away from the home. They manage to get out of the grounds, start hitchhiking, and get a lift after an hour. They get dropped about a hundred miles away from the home near the motorway and head straight for Birmingham. By the time they both manage to get back to Birmingham and arrive at Gingerbread, it's about nine o'clock in the evening.

"Tea Jay!" His mother shouts as she puts both hands over her mouth in shock at seeing her son.

"The coppers are looking for you two! Tea Jay, why did you run away, Bab?" his mother asks.

"You bleeding know why, Mom! Them bullies at the care home. I'm not going back, Mom, no way. They bully people mentally and say horrible things that bring you down. They lock you in a room called the Sin-Bin if you misbehave and make out, you're worthless. They threaten to take away our home leave if we complain. We're kids, we're not in prison," Tea Jay insists.

The following day, after going into Tea Jay's room, his mother notices he'd already gone out. Assuming they'd both done another runner, she decides to call the police and inform them they had stayed the previous night but had run off again. However, later that day, Tea Jay and his friend return to the house where the police were waiting for them.

The two lads were returned to the children's home that evening and immediately thrown into the "sin bin" with no supper. Twelve months later, Tea Jay's mother is informed that he's improved considerably and has settled into his new environment. It's now 1986, and Tea Jay is about to enter his final year of secondary school.

As part of his educational needs, Tea Jay is told he'll be moving to another home attached to Colington Court, some thirty or forty miles from where he's currently staying. The new home is a converted barn with around twelve rooms. It's two stories high, with the boys' rooms on the upper floor. The facility also has a games room, a dining hall, and a communal area where the children gather. Across from the main building, there's a smaller cottage that serves as the main office and houses the night staff's quarters.

Six months into his stay at the new home, concerns about Tea Jay's personal hygiene arise. When the issue is raised with him, Tea Jay takes it as a personal attack, assuming he's being bullied. He decides to run away again. When Tea Jay reaches his home in the Midlands, his mother quickly realizes the environment at the children's home is making him worse. Initially, she allows him to stay.

However, after speaking to staff from the children's home, she learns the real reason he ran away—they had merely addressed his hygiene issues. Two days later, a staff member arrives at Tea Jay's house to take him back to the home. But on the way, while stopping at the staff member's house to collect some personal effects, Tea Jay bolts again, hitchhiking back to the Midlands.

"What on earth are we going to do with you, Tea Jay?" his mother exclaims in frustration.

"I'll just keep running away, Mom. I swear it," Tea Jay replies.

"You're sixteen now, Tea Jay! You're going to be leaving school in a few months. Why don't you just give this place a chance? It's not going to be for much longer, I promise," his mother pleads.

"You're all the same! Everyone makes me promises, and I'm always the fool who gets hurt and lied to. It's always 'out of sight, out of mind' with you, isn't it, Mom? You've never loved me," Tea Jay shouts.

"Tea Jay, you're going back, whether you like it or not! Just give it six more months. You'll be out of school soon, come on," she implores.

"Okay... not like I've got a choice!" Tea Jay finally relents, his voice tinged with defeat.

After a few months, Tea Jay's behavior begins to improve, and he even starts to enjoy his time at the children's home. He becomes attached to a new female teacher, developing an infatuation that clouds his judgment. This attachment becomes a fleeting source of hope for Tea Jay, but deep down, he knows it will end in heartbreak.

Another new staff member, an ex-serviceman named Vini, joins the home. Tea Jay becomes intrigued by the idea of joining the army. Vini, noticing his interest, offers to help Tea Jay explore the possibility of joining. Soon, Tea Jay's enthusiasm for the military takes over his daydreams, and he envisions himself as a soldier. He believes that joining the army will solve all his problems—that it will finally bring him the respect, love, and admiration he's always craved.

Within months, Tea Jay excels through the early stages of the recruitment process, passing his fitness test, medical exam, and initial interview. All that remains is the final interview and a weekend selection process. Social services inform him that if he passes, he'll be able to return home before starting his basic training.

By the time his final interview arrives, Tea Jay is filled with a growing sense of purpose. He convinces himself that this is the answer to everything—that being in the army will transform him into the admired figure he's always imagined himself to be.

Vini reassures him, "You've passed the interview, mate. I'd bet money on it."

Tea Jay starts walking with his head held high, consumed by fantasies of his future as a decorated soldier. He boasts to his friends at Gingerbread, the one-parent group, about his upcoming training and the glorious life ahead. His confidence inflates into a massive ego as he imagines himself adorned in a crisp uniform, loved and respected by all.

But what Tea Jay doesn't understand is that the army isn't just about looking important in a uniform or receiving admiration. It's about discipline, resilience, and the harsh realities of warfare. He's blind to the possibility of being sent into war zones, facing the prospect of serious injury or even death. In his mind, he's convinced that passing basic training will be the key to finally being accepted and respected.

But Tea Jay forgets one thing—war doesn't care about how he looks in a uniform. And there are people and forces in this world who would gladly take his life just for being a soldier.

ON THE RUN

As soon as Tea Jay arrives back at the home, he feels like he's walking on a pink fluffy cloud. Nothing and no one can bring him down. Barny has assured him that he's made it into the services, and Tea Jay has convinced himself that it's a done deal. He tells everyone at the home that he's finally going home in a couple of weeks before starting basic training in the army.

But the other kids are growing tired of hearing about it.

Tea Jay walks taller than ever, head high, his heart soaring. For the first time in his life, he feels accepted. Society has embraced him, or so he believes. He can't stop the adrenaline rushing through his veins.

"I'm fuckin' buzzing! What a trip, the government trusts someone like me to protect the country. No one can bring me down now," Tea Jay boasts to the other lads.

"I'm better than these kids because I'm in the army. I'm better than these idiots in here. The sooner I start training, the better—I'll be shot of this care system and these wankers for good," he thinks to himself.

"How do you know you got in? They haven't written you yet. Haha, I bet you haven't even been accepted, you fucker!" one of the kids taunts, smirking.

"I have been accepted. Barny even told the manager he'd bet money on it. Barny knows his stuff, he's been in the army," Tea Jay snaps back, fire rising in his chest.

"Oh really? Barny knows everything, does he?" the other boy jeers, shaking his head.

"He knows more than you, you prick!" Tea Jay snarls, his fists clenched.

Barney is everything Tea Jay wants to be. At 26, he's fit, good-looking, and always seems to have it together. He's the kind of guy everyone in the home respects, from the kids to the staff. A former corporal and PTI in the army, Barney carries himself with a quiet confidence. His posture is perfect, his movements fluid, and he has a charm that even the girls in the home notice, making him a magnet for admiration. Tea Jay, in particular, idolizes him. To Tea Jay, Barney represents strength, freedom from fear, and an escape from the abuse he's endured. Barney's presence is a reminder of what Tea Jay could be—confident, strong, and respected. It's this admiration that makes Tea Jay want to join the army, not for the honour or discipline, but to become someone like Barney, someone who seemed immune to pain and fear.

A week later, after returning from home leave, Tea Jay is called into the office. Barny stands there, along with one of the home's managers, a large brown envelope in hand. Tea Jay can feel his heart pounding as they pass him the letter.

Barny's eyes avoid his. Tea Jay tears open the envelope, his hands trembling slightly. His eyes land on the cold words of rejection.

Dear Mr. T Jay,

We would like to thank you for your interest in joining the armed forces. However, on this occasion, your application has been unsuccessful.

We recommend that you consider gaining insight into the Armed Services by joining the Territorial Army before reapplying.

We welcome any future application to join the armed services within six months of this letter.

Sincerely,

An Officer

The words hit Tea Jay like a hammer. His chest tightens. His legs feel weak. Everything he'd built up, the future he'd imagined, crumbles in an instant. His vision blurs as tears start to sting his eyes.

Barny and the manager look at him with sympathetic expressions, but they might as well be ghosts. Tea Jay feels the weight of embarrassment sinking in. He's devastated, shattered. Every bit of confidence, all the high hopes he'd allowed himself to believe in, vanishes. He has no backup plan. No plan B.

The manager speaks up, breaking the silence. "This means your discharge is postponed, Tea Jay. You won't be leaving in a couple of weeks."

Tea Jay's heart sinks even further. His head feels heavy, and his breathing grows shallow. "Why can't I go home?" he demands, his voice cracking. Tears flow freely now, a mix of anger, shame, and deep sorrow.

"We all agreed that the army would have been a great move for you, Tea Jay," Barny begins, his voice steady but with a hint of regret. "It really would've been a fantastic career for you. We were ready to step back, knowing you had a strong path ahead. But without a job to go to, no college courses lined up, and no qualifications in hand, we think it's in your best interest to stay with us for at least another six months, or at least until you're seventeen."

Tea Jay listens in silence, his heart sinking further with every word.

One of the other lads, noticing the change in Tea Jay, begins to make trouble. He's not his usual cheery self, not the bragging kid they'd gotten used to, and they start picking at the wound.

"What's wrong with you, Tea Jay? Got a face like a slapped arse!" one of the boys sneers. "Ah, I know what it is—you got a knock-back from the army, didn't you? Ha, ha! You wanker! Hey, everyone, guess what? Soldier boy here got rejected from the army. I told ya! Set yourself up for a fall, didn't ya? Serves you right, you wanker!"

The words cut deep, but Tea Jay doesn't fight back. He walks around the home aimlessly, feeling lost and broken. His mind replays every step of the army application process, wondering where he went wrong. The rejection gnaws at him, eating away at his self-worth.

"Why didn't I get in? What went wrong?" the questions haunt him relentlessly, circling his mind like vultures.

The army was his only hope, the one thing that would have made him feel important. Without it, he's adrift, struggling to find a reason to keep going. Suicidal thoughts creep into his mind like shadows he can't shake.

It's now October, five long months since the rejection letter, and Tea Jay's life feels stuck on pause. But there's one silver lining: he's about to turn seventeen, and Bonfire Night is just around the corner. He's excited, not for the fireworks, but because he's been told he'll finally be discharged from full-time care.

To celebrate, Tea Jay goes to the local village with a few of the other lads from the home and one of the staff members. He heads to the pub, knowing the staff turn a blind eye when it comes to the kids from the home. He orders a lager and lime, then another. And soon, he's lost count. The alcohol dulls the ache, letting him forget for a little while.

A week later, Tea Jay's ecstatic as he leaves the home with his social worker. They take him to a self-contained hostel in Birmingham. For the first time in his life, he's free, on his own.

But freedom comes with a price.

He has no life skills. He can't cook, budget, save, or even wash or iron his clothes. The staff at the home had tried to teach him, encouraged him to open bank accounts and start saving, but Tea Jay had always shrugged it off. Now, those choices weigh heavily on him.

The very next day, Tea Jay gets his first £150 giro from the Department of Health & Social Security. For a moment, he's on that pink fluffy cloud again, feeling invincible. It's nearly Christmas 1987, and he's got money in his pocket and a growing taste for booze.

For a few days, Tea Jay feels like a bird released from a cage after years of confinement. He's free, flying high. But deep down, the same old emptiness gnaws at him. He longs to feel liked, loved, and accepted—he yearns for someone to take care of him.

But as the days go on, reality slowly creeps in. He's alone, adrift in a world that expects him to fend for himself, and Tea Jay isn't sure how much longer he can keep pretending that everything's alright.

Tea Jay feels utterly broken. His mental health issues have plagued him since early childhood, leaving him feeling like a teenager who's had his heart ripped out, trampled upon, and discarded. There's a gaping void where his self-worth should be, and he believes he's beyond repair—kicked to the curb by social services like a broken machine, deemed irreparable.

He's confused, isolated, and burdened by feelings of abandonment. Whenever a woman offers him kindness or friendship, he doesn't know how to respond. With no loving female role model to draw upon, his inexperience and deep-seated issues of abandonment surface, attaching all his painful emotions to those women. It's too much, and he ends up pushing them away, trapped in a cycle of confusion and insecurity.

His mother warns him about his spending. "You're not in care anymore, Tea Jay. You've got to be smart about your money." She reminds him that the family is going on holiday in six months and that he should start saving now.

But Tea Jay feels distant from them. He's somewhat grateful to be going on holiday with his family, yet he feels like an outsider, disconnected from the warmth of the familial bond. The years of resentment fester inside him, a constant reminder that no amount of making up for lost time can ever repair the damage he feels has already been done.

"I'll be fine. The holiday's ages away, plenty of time to save," Tea Jay tells himself, brushing off his mother's advice.

The next day, Tea Jay wakes up with no recollection of the night before. His pockets are empty, not a penny to his name. His cupboards are bare, his stomach gnawing with hunger, and he hasn't even got the bus fare to visit his mom.

One of the other lads at the hostel gives him an idea: "Go to the police station, tell 'em you lost your wallet. Then hit up the DHSS and apply for a Crisis loan. Tell them you've lost everything."

"No, I'd get caught. I can't do that. I'll ask my social worker," Tea Jay replies, unsure of what to do.

Later that same day, his social worker delivers a blow Tea Jay wasn't prepared for: he's being discharged from the care order that's governed his life for the past ten years. Once he leaves the care of social services, he's on his own—no more financial or emotional support. The safety net he's relied on is about to disappear.

As the weeks pass, Tea Jay's fear and confusion deepen. He's institutionalized, used to being looked after, and the thought of navigating life on his own terrifies him. When he's evicted from his hostel for drunkenly destroying some furniture, he's got nowhere to turn. Desperate, he asks his mom if he can stay with her.

By the summer of 1988, Tea Jay's spiraling out of control. His mother and uncle Rob have repeatedly urged him to save money for their upcoming holiday, but he can't seem to hold on to a penny. Whatever he gets is quickly spent on booze, burning a hole in his pocket before he knows it.

The day arrives when Tea Jay, Lacey, Uncle Rob, Nanny Lou, and his mother are set to board a coach for the 36-hour journey from London to Salou, Spain. Tea Jay's excitement is tempered by the weight of his addiction, but he's doing his best to keep it under wraps.

As they're about to board, his mother pulls him aside. "You need help with your drinking, Tea Jay."

Her words feel like a slap in the face, and Tea Jay is mortified. In front of everyone, she's laid bare his most vulnerable flaw. Years of anger, frustration, and resentment bubble to the surface, and Tea Jay's tongue becomes a weapon, sharp and unforgiving.

"You owe me more than money could ever buy," he spits through gritted teeth, his face turning red with fury. His mother stands silent, tears forming in her eyes, but Tea Jay can't stop. His words, like molten lava, pour out uncontrollably, scalding her with each bitter syllable. Tears stream down his own face, soaking his shirt, but the flood of emotion is too powerful to rein in.

As he rips into her, all of his unresolved pain—years of feeling unloved, abandoned, and broken—surge forward, leaving him raw, exposed, and hurting.

"Tut! How dare you label me as an alcoholic. Just because you and that weirdo Uncle Richard are alcoholics doesn't give you the right to call me one." Tea Jay snaps, his voice heavy with bitterness. "Besides, don't you think it's a little too late to start moralizing now?"

His words cut like glass. "I needed you ten years ago, Mom. Before you lied, sacrificed me, and sent me to Charles Burns. Don't start putting on the caring mother act now. And don't even try throwing this holiday in my face. It was Uncle Rob and Nanny who paid for it, not you." His anger reverberates through the room.

His mother, visibly shaken, fires back. "So why is it you never have any money? Why've you been arrested twice this month for being drunk and disorderly?"

"Because I never had a real mother to guide me!" Tea Jay explodes. "You abandoned me! You let me rot in that place and then lied about me. You threw me to the dogs!" His voice, filled with anguish and fury, echoes through the room.

Two days into their holiday, Tea Jay and his family go out for the night in Salou. Tea Jay's attention is quickly caught by Helen, a stunning British waitress from up north. He's immediately smitten, but there's a problem: Helen's already got a boyfriend stationed with the armed forces in Germany. Undeterred, Tea Jay tries to impress her, spinning a tale about his own plans to join the army.

"If you didn't have a boyfriend, would you consider going out with me?" he asks, trying to sound nonchalant but feeling a knot form in his stomach.

Helen gives him a warm smile, her Sheffield accent soft. "Ooh, I don't know."

That's all it takes. Tea Jay's mind races. Her smile becomes a green light in his head, and he's hooked. He imagines that smile meaning something more—hope. The kind of hope he's always longed for: to be liked, loved, and accepted. That smile becomes a beacon for his desire to be seen, to matter.

For Tea Jay, who's never been used to this kind of attention from girls his age, the feeling is intoxicating. Suddenly, Helen becomes more than just a pretty face—she's the promise of something he's craved all his life: acceptance. His mind spins a fantasy where the young waitress becomes his future.

Tea Jay is in Salou for two weeks with little more than twenty pounds, which he's already spent. Desperate to impress Helen, he rifles through his Uncle Rob's jeans and steals five thousand pesetas, roughly twenty-five pounds. He puts on a brand-new white suit, hoping it will catch her attention, and heads back to Garfield's in the sweltering afternoon heat, eager for another glimpse of her.

When he arrives at the restaurant, heads turn. Helen smiles, but it's more of a chuckle as she looks at his outfit.

"It's four o'clock in the afternoon and thirty degrees outside. Why are you wearing a white suit? You look like you're about to dance in Saturday Night Fever," she says, teasing him with a grin.

Tea Jay's face flushes beetroot red as the attention of the room centres on him. Embarrassed but still trying to save face, he stammers, "I wore it for you... Don't you like it?"

Helen smiles kindly but firmly replies, "I've already told you; I've got a boyfriend."

That evening, a couple of hours later, Tea Jay is well on his way to getting drunk. He's not only spent his uncle's five thousand pesetas but also met an acquaintance who's been buying him pints. By the time his family approaches Garfield's a few hours later, Tea Jay is in a bad state—slaughtered and crying his eyes out because Helen has told him she's not interested.

"Tea Jay, you fall in love too quick. You've always been like this," his mother says with a sigh.

"Come on, I'll take you back to the apartment to sleep it off," Rob offers, trying to get him out of public view.

Back at the apartment, Rob eyes him closely and asks, "Did you take a five thousand peseta note out of my jeans while I was in the shower? I bet it was you, you little Barstard."

"No, Rob! I wouldn't do that to you, no way," Tea Jay protests with a drunken hiccup.

"I know it was you, you Barstard," Rob says, but with a grin this time.

"Sorry, Rob..." Tea Jay admits as he begins to sober up later in the evening.

"I knew it!" Rob says, laughing but shaking his head. "You Barstard."

When they arrive back home after the holiday, Tea Jay's mother tells him he can live with her—on the condition that he pays her at least £10 a week from his dole money.

By summer 1989, Tea Jay receives a credit card in the post, excited to see he's been granted a £500 credit limit. His first thought is wild: he could use it to go back to Salou, back to Helen. But then he shakes his head, realizing that whole thing was just a fantasy.

Within two weeks, Tea Jay has blown through his £500 credit limit and is £750 overdrawn. His card is swiftly withdrawn by the bank. Desperate, he starts applying for store cards everywhere, convinced they'll be easier to get. He doesn't want the goods—just the money he can make from selling them for booze.

Eighteen months later, Tea Jay's drinking has skyrocketed. He's buried in thousands of pounds of debt. His mother has kicked him out because debt collectors won't stop knocking on her door. To make matters worse, he's on the run, wanted by the police for various offences ranging from drunk and disorderly to fraud—anything to get more booze.

Deep down, all Tea Jay really wants is to be liked, loved, and accepted. But he's chasing it in all the wrong ways. He believes that looking good will make him feel good, and that money will impress the right woman, who will fill the gaping hole in his soul. But he has no understanding of self-worth or self-esteem. Everything he does is a frantic attempt to escape the pain he carries.

One day, Tea Jay bumps into his brother Jay and an acquaintance named Pea. Jay asks him if he wants to come for a drink, and Tea Jay leaps at the opportunity—Jay rarely invites him along to anything with his friends.

After a few too many drinks, Pea turns to Jay and says, "Fancy going for a spin in the Sierra Cosworth? I nicked it earlier today."

Jay shakes his head. "Nah, mate. I'm already wanted by the cops for a few burglaries. I'm not looking to add car theft to the list."

But Tea Jay, desperate for any form of excitement or acceptance, jumps at the chance. "I'm in," he says, and climbs into the front passenger seat without a second thought.

Pea laughs as he throws the car into gear and wheel-spins across the park and onto the road. "Let's have a bit of fun with the old bill," he says, grinning as the tires screech and the car rockets forward.

"What are you going to do, Pea?" Tea Jay asks nervously as his stomach churns with fear. He suddenly regrets getting into the stolen car.

All Tea Jay wants to do is get out of the car, but fear keeps him silent. Something dark and sinister hovers around Pea, his brother's friend, and Tea Jay senses it now more than ever. Despite the panic rising inside him, he doesn't say a word. All he's ever wanted is to be liked and accepted, especially since he's felt so lonely for so long.

Pea slams the car into top gear and speeds down the road, deciding to give the police a chase. The stolen car zooms past a Mini with two unsuspecting elderly occupants at a reckless 85 mph, nearly tipping their car onto two wheels.

Tea Jay's adrenaline surges as fear grips him tighter. Sweat soaks his shirt, and his breathing becomes shallow and rapid. He feels like his heart is going to explode out of his chest.

"Pea, I need a few pints after this," Tea Jay blurts out nervously.

They manage to lose the police, eventually hiding the stolen car. Despite the chaos, they have the audacity to call for a taxi to take them back to the pub where they first got into the stolen car.

A couple of days later, Pea changes the plates on the car. They park up in the countryside, on a restaurant car park. It's pouring rain, but Pea still plans to sell some parts from the stolen car to his brother, who owns the same model.

Suddenly, without warning, several cars screech to a halt, surrounding them. Voices scream at the top of their lungs.

"Armed police! Get your hands in the air!"

Tea Jay's heart sinks. Both he and the others are ordered out of the cars one by one and forced to lie face-down on the wet ground. Their hands are cable-tied behind their backs.

Tea Jay's mind races. "We only had a stolen motor and a chase. Armed police? What the hell is going on?" he thinks.

At the police station, Tea Jay, Pea, and the others are informed they're under arrest for conspiracy to commit armed robbery. Tea Jay's confusion deepens as the situation escalates beyond anything he could have imagined.

They are kept isolated from one another, with a radio blaring in the walkway between the cells to prevent them from talking.

The next day, during questioning, the police turn Tea Jay's mother's house upside down. They dig through the back garden, removing plastic tubing hidden beneath the dirt and rubble. The police suggest that large amounts of cash may have been hidden inside the tubes, trying to pin additional charges on the brothers.

A few days later, while still in custody, Tea Jay sees the front page of the local paper. It reads:

"Seven Quizzed Over Post Office Robberies"

Tea Jay's stomach drops again. What started as a reckless joyride has turned into something far more serious.

On the third day of their detention, Tea Jay and his brother sit down with their solicitor. The lawyer looks concerned, his face grim.

"Where do you know this bloke, Pea, from?" the solicitor asks them both. His tone is more serious than before.

The solicitor goes on to inform them that Pea is well-known to the authorities—a career criminal wanted up and down the country, notorious for driving in armed robberies.

Tea Jay sits in stunned silence, realizing the gravity of the situation. What seemed like a reckless thrill has spiralled into something that could ruin his life.

"I met him through Jay last week. He offered me some drinks, and afterwards he asked if I wanted to have a laugh with the police. I felt obliged because he bought me booze, so I said yes," Tea Jay tells his solicitor.

The solicitor sighs. "Would you jump off a bridge if he told you to, Tea Jay? Anyway, you're both going to receive section 47/3 bail and will have to come back for further questioning. They'll decide if you'll be charged with conspiracy to rob."

The solicitor then turns serious. "Unfortunately, Tea Jay, the police are keeping you in custody because you're wanted on a no-bail warrant in magistrates' court. You'll probably be held until Monday, then taken to court for sentencing."

Tea Jay ends up with a six-month custodial sentence and is sent to a young offenders' institution.

On his second night inside, he's placed in a cell with someone serving many years for armed robbery and another inmate doing seven years for aggravated burglary. He's terrified, but he knows he can't show it—something he's learned from his brother, Jay. Fear in prison is a sign of weakness, and weakness is dangerous here.

Tea Jay's cell is tiny, about 6.5 square meters. The walls are painted a dingy, dirty cream, and there are two single beds with thin, uncomfortable mattresses. The bedding consists of lime-green sheets and a scratchy blanket. A foam pillow completes the setup. There's an emergency bell on the left-hand side of the iron door and a small, barred window. There's also a slop bucket for relieving themselves during the 23 hours they're locked up in the cell. Tea Jay knows all too well that prison is no fairytale.

As he walks around the exercise yard, he sees other inmates picking up cigarette butts from the ground, rolling them into new smokes. The guards glance at them with disgust, then look away. They turn a blind eye to a prisoner getting hit over the head with a sock full of batteries, but the riot bell screams when a fight breaks out over a roll-up cigarette. Suddenly, guards seem to materialize from every direction.

The constant stench of bleach and cleaning fluids clings to the air wherever Tea Jay goes in the prison. It's a stark reminder of the grim reality inside.

"What you in for?" the burglar asks Tea Jay one evening.

"Fraud," Tea Jay says, trying to keep his voice steady.

"You shaking, mate? You scared?" the burglar presses. "Don't be scared in here. Show weakness, and you'll end up being someone's bitch, or worse. In prison, weakness is a big no-no."

"I'm not scared. Just got bad nerves," Tea Jay explains. "I was scalded with boiling water when I was a kid."

The burglar doesn't press further, but Tea Jay can't shake the feeling of being an outsider. Two weeks later, he's transferred to another prison, swearing to himself that he'll stop drinking and get a job when he gets out.

But prison life is hard. Tea Jay struggles to adjust, and he doesn't get along with the other inmates. His thoughts constantly drift to his pregnant girlfriend, and the worry gnaws at him.

Two weeks before his release, Tea Jay receives a visit from his mom, Jay, and Uncle Rob.

"Tea Jay, what's happening to you, Bab? You're drinking like it's going out of fashion. Even though it's not your child, you've got a girlfriend who's pregnant and needs your support. When are you going to stop living in the past and blaming everyone else for your issues? You need to face your demons, because unless you do, you'll always be on the run. You've been offered a fantastic opportunity when you get out of prison, by the way, but I'll only tell you about it when you get out." Tea Jay's mother says, all excited.

"Have we heard anything about the conspiracy case, Jay?" Tea Jay enquires.

"Nah, but it's not looking good." Jay sighs.

Tea Jay looks at his mother in disbelief and says: "Really? I can't believe you've just said that to me. Don't you remember when this happened to my hand? What about the fire all those years ago, Mom? What about uncle Rich then, Mom? I've been crying out for help for many years. It's just that no one has ever listened to me, have they?" Tea Jay screams, then storms off the visit.

THE BRISTOL ATTACK

"What's this wonderful opportunity you've been telling me about since I was inside, then, Mom?" Tea Jay asks sarcastically.

"Don't give me your lip, you ungrateful sod! A friend of mine runs a fairground, and he's offering you a chance to travel and work with them," his mother snaps.

"Ungrateful pissant," she thinks to herself.

"So, this is the big secret you've been hiding from me, is it? What's the pay like?" Tea Jay asks, clearly unimpressed.

"I don't know! You'll have to ask them on the fairground! I didn't have to go out of my way to try and help you, Tea Jay," his mother says, furious.

Tea Jay is simmering with resentment. He lives in a space of blame—toward his mother and certain others—and can't forgive or forget. He feels he's owed answers for everything that happened when he was a child. Lonely and afraid, he believes those people should have protected him from the psychological and physical abuse he endured. Tea Jay is terribly lost, craving guidance but feeling as though he's been left to walk this lonely road on his own.

For the life of him, he can't accept the part he played in his past. He becomes controlling, insisting on answers to questions he's carried with him for years. He still hears voices, has flashbacks of the fire, and is haunted by nightmares of the man in his room. When certain subjects are brought up, they are often pushed aside or avoided, leaving him feeling even more isolated.

So, he decides to run. To leave it all behind, he calls up his mother's friend and becomes a gaff-lad at the fairground.

Although he wants answers, Tea Jay just wants his mother to own her part and let go of whatever fear she's been clinging to for years. He yearns to forgive her, to feel validated, liked, loved, and accepted.

Though he knows working on the fairground is a dead-end job, he reasons it could help him save some money while signing on the dole—and maybe even help him find a girlfriend. But Tea Jay's severe mental health issues are always lurking in the background. He has serious attachment issues from early childhood, and his drinking problem is spiralling out of control, though he's in complete denial about it.

He's never held down a job, and money seems to melt through his fingers like snow in June.

Now, just past his twenty-second birthday, Tea Jay has been working the fairground for a while and is getting along with the other gaff-lads. But deep down, he's still trying to escape the frustration, the mental anguish, and the horrors he's felt for years. One evening, unmindful of the dangers, Tea Jay approaches one of his co-workers with excitement in his eyes.

"Yo, got any tabs left, mate?" he whispers in Brownie's ear.

"Yeah, course," Brownie replies, rummaging through his pocket while glancing around to make sure the coast is clear.

That same evening, Tea Jay leaves his trailer with one of the lads to head to the local garage. The Weed they smoked earlier has given him a serious case of the munchies.

"Have you dropped that tab yet, Tea?" Paddy asks casually.

Paddy, with his signature deep Irish accent, is a fixture at the funfair where TJ works. He's a simple guy, always wearing his well-worn green parka, no matter the weather. There's a warmth to him, a genuine appreciation for the little things in life. For Paddy, a sit-down meal isn't some grand affair; it's fish and chips, eaten right in the chippy. That's his idea of living well, and it's part of what makes him so endearing. He's a good friend to TJ, always quick with a laugh and a kind word, someone who makes even the hardest days at the fair feel a little lighter.

"Yeah, about an hour ago," Tea Jay replies, sounding disappointed and irritated. He's frustrated because nothing seems to be happening.

But just as those words leave his mouth, something strange occurs. As he approaches the petrol station kiosk, Tea Jay feels as though he's stepping onto a molehill. Confused, he glances down at his feet, but he's on solid concrete. The idea of a molehill is ridiculous, yet it felt so real.

"What the hell was that?" Tea Jay mutters, his face twisting in confusion.

"What are you on about, you madman?" Paddy laughs, clearly amused by Tea Jay's confusion.

As they head back down the hill toward their trailers, an icy fear creeps over Tea Jay, slowly wrapping itself around his mind. He feels an overwhelming sense of dread, as if something terrible is about to happen. His heart races, and beads of sweat begin to form on his forehead. The streetlamps appear unnaturally bright, almost piercing his vision, and regret begins to sink in. He wishes he'd never taken the acid. A tidal wave of panic washes over him as he questions whether he's going to be alright.

"Don't mess with me, Paddy! How bright do those streetlamps look to you, mate?" Tea Jay asks, his voice filled with panic.

"I already told ya, mate—nothing's wrong. Stop freaking out, will ya? The lights are perfectly normal," Paddy sniggers, clearly unfazed.

Later that night, despite his frantic state and his mind swirling in chaos, Tea Jay tries to sleep. But as soon as he closes his eyes, something sinister floods his vision—an evil-looking eye, dark and menacing. It's everywhere he turns, whether his eyes are open or shut. No matter what he does, he can't escape it. It feels as though something wicked is reaching into his soul, judging him. His heart pounds in terror, and he's overcome with the sensation that he's on the verge of death.

Suddenly, a deep, booming male voice fills the room. It echoes all around him, though no one else seems to hear it. The voice is suffocating, oppressive, and it fills Tea Jay with dread.

"You're going to die!" the voice bellows.

Despite how loud and menacing the voice is, the two guys sharing his trailer, still playing cards, don't seem to notice a thing.

Again and again, the voice taunts him, growing louder and more menacing with each passing moment.

"You're going to die tonight. God doesn't love you, and you've brought this on yourself."

Desperate, Tea Jay clutches onto the only thing he knows: The Lord's Prayer. He repeats it over and over in his mind, reciting it as if it might protect him from whatever this darkness is. But the fear that grips him, the judgment he feels for his past actions, tightens its hold. Every word feels hollow, as though mocking his past mistakes, particularly how he used to laugh at his R.E. teacher back in school.

His heart thunders in his chest, growing louder with every beat. In desperation, he turns to the guys sharing his trailer.

Tea Jay's growing paranoia, mixed with the haunting voices in his head, reaches a fever pitch as he tells the two guys in the trailer, "I think I'm going to die."

The guys look at him, then at each other, shaking their heads and laughing in disbelief, clearly not taking him seriously.

But for Tea Jay, something strange and unexpected happens. Just as he finishes speaking, he feels an unfamiliar sensation—a deep, calming peace unlike anything he's ever experienced. While he tries to process this sudden change, he hears another voice, softer and more soothing than the previous one.

"Tea Jay, it's okay! You're just panicking; it's just an illusion of the drug. You're going to be okay this time. Don't worry, everything's going to be just fine."

The words settle over him like a blanket, easing his racing mind and pounding heart. For the first time that night, he feels grounded. Then, the female voice speaks again, even softer this time, but more impactful.

"Tea Jay, this path you're taking is not for you. Drugs aren't for you! Ask for help, and it shall be given. I promise."

Those words stay with him, lingering in his thoughts over the next few weeks. He can't shake the two distinct voices from that night. The booming, ominous one that had filled him with terror, and the soft, calming one that brought peace.

"What the hell was that all about?" Tea Jay ponders again and again. "Where did those voices come from? And what did she mean by, 'Ask for help and it shall be given?'"

No matter how much he tries to push the thoughts away, they keep flooding back. He questions whether there had been anyone else in the trailer besides the two guys. Could it have been something else entirely? His mind drifts toward possibilities he's never seriously considered before.

"Could that have been...?" he starts to wonder, but quickly shuts the thought down, laughing at himself. "People would think I've gone mad if they heard me talking like this," he mutters under his breath. "Bleeding idiot, Tea Jay!"

Yet despite his attempts to dismiss it as just a bad trip, the idea lingers. The voice had brought such calm, and something deep inside him whispers that the peace it gave could only have come from something divine. He toys with the thought: was it God?

Weeks later, Tea Jay meets a girl named Jane on the fairground. After one night together, he falls head over heels, typical of his habit of forming instant, intense attachments. Jane, however, is from a different circuit, one that doesn't visit the same parks as his. Desperate not to lose her, Tea Jay asks if her showman is looking for workers. Much to his delight, they are, and Tea Jay eagerly jumps at the chance to join her circuit.

But it isn't long before things fall apart. After a row with Jane, she kicks him out of her trailer, and his new boss—who Tea Jay accuses of sleeping with Jane—fires him.

Now, Tea Jay finds himself in Bristol, homeless and penniless. Though lost, he is still streetwise enough to know how to work the system. Realizing he's owed two weeks' worth of dole money, he heads to the Social Security office and spins a story about being a New Age Traveller, moving between free music festivals and fairs. The trick works, and he picks up around sixty pounds for the two weeks of unpaid money.

With the cash in hand, he manages to find a temporary bed at a homeless hostel. But within weeks, Tea Jay is back on the streets,

broke, and standing in front of the Magistrates Court for attempting
to obtain money by deception.

Miraculously, he's granted bail and sent to stay in a bail hostel. But
even as he navigates these highs and lows, those voices from that night
in the trailer continue to echo in his mind.

Tea Jay has been in Bristol for about three months. He's made a
few acquaintances, but none he'd truly call friends. One night, one of
those acquaintances invites him over for a smoke. Tea Jay agrees and
ends up at Dick's flat, along with another guy, all gathered to smoke
weed.

From the moment Tea Jay steps inside the flat, a sense of unease
creeps over him, but he dismisses it as paranoia from the weed. The
flat is on the second floor, and the stench of stale food hits him immediately. It smells like wet cardboard, old varnish, and dirty socks.

Still, Tea Jay isn't concerned about the mess. He's just there for
a free smoke and a few cans of booze. The wooden floors are bare,
and the three-piece suit is covered with a grimy cream throw. Graffiti
stains the yellowing, damp walls. In one corner, a dirty two-hob oven
sits atop a grimy surface. The coffee table in the centre of the room is
cluttered with Rizlas, loose tobacco, empty cigarette butts, and a bong.

After about an hour, the mood in the room suddenly shifts.

"Where's the fuckin' weed gone off the table?" Dick shouts.

"I haven't touched your fuckin' weed, honest," Tea Jay shouts back,
feeling defensive.

"There was a fuckin' eighth on the bastard table! Where the fuck's
it gone?" Dick screams as he suddenly smacks Tea Jay in the jaw.

Stunned and shaken, Tea Jay barely has time to react. Dick gets up
in his face, forcing him back onto the sofa. Tea Jay is terrified as Dick
laughs while sitting on top of him. Another acquaintance, standing

nearby, asks if Dick needs help, but Dick just laughs, telling him no. They all find the situation amusing—except for Tea Jay.

"I haven't touched your sodding weed, I swear! Get off me and let me up!" Tea Jay shouts in panic.

"I don't give a fuck! You're still going to pay me in some way for the weed I've lost," Dick threatens.

"I haven't got any money; I've got absolutely fuck all," Tea Jay replies, his voice trembling as the reality of the situation sets in.

Later that night, Tea Jay is numb and in shock, unable to process what has just happened. He's shaking and panicking, trying to find a way out. His attacker has locked him inside the flat and loosely tied him up before leaving for another flat. Tea Jay's trainers have been taken to prevent him from running, but he couldn't care less about his shoes.

Desperate, Tea Jay smashes a window with his fist, severing a vein in the process. Blood starts pouring from his wrist, and soon he feels faint. He manages to drop to the ground but twists his ankle when he hits the bottom.

As he hobbles up a hill, he hears a familiar voice calling after him. Confused and weak, he can't tell if it's his attacker or someone else he knows. The voice gets closer and closer as Tea Jay struggles to climb the steep hill. Blood soaks his clothes, and he can't run because of his injured ankle. Feeling too weak, he collapses in the middle of the road and passes out.

THE WINEPRESS & THE VINYARD

Tea Jay finds himself on a cluttered, deserted island. The sun is shining on a warm, lovely day. Off in the distance, just beyond the deep blue waters, lies a spotless beach, bustling with activity. He gazes out toward the beach and sees groups of happy-looking people, their laughter carried faintly on the breeze.

There's something familiar about them, something deep within him stirs, yet he can't quite place where he's seen them before.

"How is it possible to know someone, to recognize their faces, and yet be sure I've never met them before?" Tea Jay wonders, confusion creeping over him.

As he looks at the inviting, crystal-clear water, he feels a fleeting sense of peace. The water sparkles like glass, revealing the depths below. He watches as people dive in, their faces glowing with elation as they disappear beneath the surface. But even as he witnesses their joy, a heavy weight lingers in his chest. He feels unclean, unworthy, and afraid.

One man in the water catches his eye—a Middle Eastern-looking figure, in his late twenties or early thirties. The man's gaze locks onto Tea Jay, and suddenly, words flash before his eyes:

"Come on, jump in! Don't be afraid; you'll be safe, I promise. If you need help, just ask."

Tea Jay's mind races. Am I dreaming? How can someone talk to me without saying a word? Am I dead?

The man shakes his head, as if reading Tea Jay's thoughts, and points toward a rollercoaster on a distant pier. As Tea Jay's eyes follow the man's gesture, fear begins to grip him. The fairground ride twists and turns, moving relentlessly forward and backward, its chaotic motion mirroring the confusion and chaos in his own life. The man's gaze intensifies, and Tea Jay feels the weight of his words without hearing them.

"This is your life, Tea Jay. You need to ask for help."

Suddenly, a distant voice pierces the dreamlike scene.

"Tea Jay, wake up! Mr. Jay! Tea Jay, are you with us?"

The sound yanks him back to reality. His eyes open, and the vibrant island fades away. He's no longer in a peaceful place but finds himself handcuffed to a hospital bed, a police officer standing beside him. The harshness of the fluorescent lights above stings his eyes, and everything feels too real.

Confusion and rage surge through him. His body is weak, his head spinning.

"What the hell is going on? What have I done wrong?" Tea Jay demands, his voice hoarse and filled with frustration.

"Calm down, Mr. Jay," a concerned nurse responds. "You're lucky to be alive. We thought we'd lost you."

Tea Jay stares at her in disbelief, the nurse's words echoing in his mind.

"Lost me? What does she mean, they thought they'd lost me?"

"You actually died for a few minutes," the police officer explains, his tone firm but gentle.

Tea Jay blinks, trying to process the words. He remembers the island, the man in the water, the piercing voice. Was it real? Was it just a dream?

"You're handcuffed because you're wanted on multiple charges," the officer continues. "Fraud. You've got a couple of warrants out for your arrest in Birmingham, not backed for bail."

Tea Jay's anger flares again, but this time it's coupled with a gnawing sense of hopelessness. His mind flashes back to the night before. He remembers the fear, the humiliation, the desperate escape from his attacker. His body tenses under the covers as shame washes over him.

"I don't want to talk about it," Tea Jay mutters, burying his tear-streaked face in the pillow. "Just tell me what I've done wrong."

The officer watches him closely, concern etched into his expression. "Last night, you were found in the middle of the road. You were in nothing but boxer shorts and a shirt. You were bleeding heavily. Judging by the cuts on your wrist, it looks like you broke a window to escape from somewhere."

Tea Jay can't hold back anymore. "I wish he'd killed me," he mutters, his voice thick with raw emotion. "It would've been easier."

The officer's eyes soften. He can see that this young man has been through hell. "This kid's broken," he thinks to himself. "There's more to this than he's saying."

Slowly, Tea Jay begins to open up, recounting how he was lured into that flat, how he had trusted his attacker, and how it all went wrong. But as he gets to the hardest part, his voice falters, the words sticking in his throat. The shame and terror are too overwhelming to face, let alone speak.

Fear of being judged holds him back.

The officer softly asks.

"Are you trying to say…?"

However, the officer is suddenly interrupted.

"What do you think; you're the copper," Tea Jay says under his breath.

"You need to say what happened and be willing to make a statement, Tea Jay," the Police Officer says softly.

Hopelessness is written all over Tea Jay's face as he turns over and faces the other way, quietly saying so no one else could hear under a veil of tears and deep sadness.

"I was assaulted."

"We'll get our doctor to examine you right away. If you get bail, you'll need to contact us to make a formal statement. If you're remanded in custody, you can write to us requesting a Special Visit from the Police to make a statement. My name's P.C J. Jones," the officer says.

It's now a week after the incident in Bristol and Tea Jay has been taken back to Birmingham to face a warrant for failing to appear in court. Although Tea Jay expects to be remanded in custody, he still tries his luck with a desperate attempt for bail. However, the Stipendiary magistrate has none of it and remands him in custody for six weeks to appear at Crown Court for sentencing.

It's 1993 and Tea Jay is back in jail in the prison reception waiting to be processed. He knows it's going to be hours before he gets to the wing.

"There's the medical, the strip search, and all the intrusive stupid questions," he thinks to himself.

He has the all too familiar sense of fear of the other inmates around him. There's also the very familiar smell of bleach and cleaning fluids that never leaves the prison.

Now he's back inside, he thinks to himself, "If I show any weakness in here, I'm screwed, and I'll become someone's gopher or worse."

Tea Jay's cell is the same old six-point five square meters. The cell walls are painted a dirty-looking creamy gloss bearing different in-mates' names and dates. There are the same old two single beds opposite each other with very thin navy-blue mattresses, lime green sheets, a green blanket, and a pillow made of foam. There's an emergency bell on the left-hand side of the cast iron door to the cell with a sarcastic message saying: "Press for service."

There's also a very small window with iron bars across it. There's a bucket for each prisoner for "slopping out." This means you have to relieve yourself in the bucket and take it out in the morning, and you're locked up for twenty-three hours a day.

Prison's no fairy tale world.

Tea Jay receives a distressing letter a fortnight later explaining that the Police have decided not to press charges against his attacker. This is because, on examination by the Police surgeon, they concluded that there's no sufficient evidence to clarify internal trauma or that force was used.

Tea Jay feels like scum, sick and mortified, and regrets making the statement because, after receiving the letter, he feels ten times worse than when the incident occurred.

"For crying out loud, if anyone sees this, I'll lose it," he mutters to himself.

Paca, Tea Jay's cellmate, asks him what's wrong. Being unaware of Tea Jay's situation, he asks him if he'd like a woman to write to.

Tea Jay says, "Yeah, why not!"

Tea Jay is excited and starts to write to a girl called Frida. After a couple of weeks, she gets a visiting order but doesn't show up at the prison. However, after another fortnight, they both agree that if Tea Jay gets Judge & Chambers and gets out, they'd love to meet up for a drink.

Tea Jay doesn't want to mess things up with this girl. However, she's unaware of his attachment and abandonment issues, which date back to his early childhood.

He's often felt punished, all alone, and not good enough. Most of the time, whenever someone Tea Jay has grown fond of enters his life, dark and fearful memories awaken, and the incredibly frightened, abandoned little boy reappears, often causing him to mess things up.

Something deep within has a desperate need to be rescued, yet it seems lost in a very dark place.

Whenever Tea Jay meets a girl, he really likes, he's notorious for scaring them off. He becomes unhealthily attached and obsessively calls them day & night. He just wants to feel liked, loved, and accepted, but every time a girl smiles at him or shows interest, he becomes fearful if he doesn't hear from her for a day. His heart aches and pounds with an insatiable unhealthy yearning for validation, because he suddenly feels he's going to be abandoned again.

It's the following Friday, and a prison officer opens Tea Jay's door to inform him he's got Judge in Chambers and to pack his kit because he's going home. Tea Jay is absolutely buzzing with excitement. He's got a grin like a Cheshire cat, and nothing can get him down. He's determined—this time will be different. He's only going to have a few beers, no more than that, before he meets Frida. But as soon as he's released, he can't resist that familiar voice in his head whispering:

"Go on, just have a couple. You deserve it after everything. Besides, you're not an alcoholic—you're too young for that."

He believes the lie, because he has no defence against that first drink. The moment he takes it, the drink takes him. The alcohol lights him up like a fifty-foot Christmas tree. He feels invincible, seven feet tall. The booze gives him the confidence he lacks, allowing him to approach Frida as if he has his life together. Frida, blindsided by Tea Jay's charm and physical attraction, doesn't see through his facade.

A month passes, and Tea Jay and Frida begin to grow closer, developing a real relationship. Frida invites him to her father's house for dinner on Sunday. Tea Jay's nerves get the better of him, and he drinks to calm himself down. He calls it "Dutch courage," but in truth, it's another excuse to drink.

Her father's house is in the suburbs, a comfortable four-bedroomed semi-detached. The moment they arrive, Frida's dad offers Tea Jay a drink, but not the kind he expects.

"How about some of my speciality fruit tea?" her father asks, smiling.

Tea Jay forces a smile, masking his disappointment. "Uh, no thanks. I'll just have a coffee, please."

He follows Frida and her father through the house. The hallway has a regal-red carpet and walls painted in cream, adorned with framed pictures of famous public speakers. They walk through to the kitchen—a modern, brown oak design with the faint smell of freshly baked bread filling the air. The open-plan lounge is filled with the distant sound of a football match on the TV.

Tea Jay's stomach growls, and he thinks, an egg sandwich with a heap of Daddy's sauce would go down perfectly right now.

As they settle into the lounge, Frida's father looks at Tea Jay seriously. "My daughter tells me you've had a bit of a chequered past—spent time in prison."

Tea Jay feels his face heat up, embarrassment prickling at his skin. He braces himself for judgment, but Frida's dad surprises him.

"Well, that's the past," her father continues. "I'm prepared to take you as I find you." His eyes soften. "Have you been drinking today, Tea Jay?"

Tea Jay hesitates, then nods. "Yeah. I'll admit it. I needed a bit of Dutch courage before meeting you, sir. Just nerves, you know?"

Her father studies him for a moment before asking, "Has alcohol been a problem for you before? I'd like to know my daughter's safe, that's all."

Tea Jay's heart pounds. Safe? He can hardly keep himself together, let alone someone else. But he tries to brush it off. "I've had a bit of a rough patch, yeah. But I'm not an alcoholic. I'm only twenty-three. I can slow down if I really try."

Her father raises an eyebrow. "Ever thought of asking God for help?"

Tea Jay scoffs internally, but keeps his expression neutral. God? What's God ever done for me? he thinks bitterly. He doesn't voice it, though, out of respect for Frida's father.

The conversation shifts, and soon enough, Frida's dad invites them both to church the following Sunday. "Come to service at Sutton Coldfield Vineyard with me. Afterward, we'll have lunch."

Tea Jay isn't thrilled about the idea, but Frida's excited, so he agrees to go. Deep down, his insecurity is gnawing at him—he's terrified of losing her, so he'll go wherever she wants just to keep her by his side.

When Sunday arrives, Tea Jay finds himself sitting in a crowded church. The assembly hall is packed, the atmosphere buzzing with energy. As they enter, the faint smell of wet paint lingers in the cloak-room, and the hall is filled with the sound of worship, people singing passionately. Tea Jay shifts in his seat, feeling out of place.

The chairs are old, wooden things, uncomfortable and likely to splinter. Tea Jay's stomach grumbles as he notices the table at the back with tea, coffee, and donuts. I should've eaten breakfast, he thinks, regretting his earlier decision to skip it.

Tea Jay really doesn't know where to put his face. Somehow, although he's fully clothed and clean on the outside, he feels naked and filthy. For some reason, Tea Jay feels really uneasy, as if everyone, including the pastor, can see straight through him.

As the Pastor gives his sermon, Tea Jay starts to feel clammy and full of fear, and begins having what he believes is a panic attack. He feels a familiar presence that he's only ever felt once before in a dream. As Pastor David speaks and delivers his message, Tea Jay is convinced his past has been revealed because the pastor's voice seems to pierce his spirit and convict him. He feels the same heavy presence flow all around him, through him, like an overwhelming tide.

Frida, I don't feel well. Can we go home, please? T.J. asks, his voice trembling.

"Is everything okay? Can I help?" David, the pastor, asks, noticing TJ's distress. His voice is calm and warm, instantly putting TJ at ease. There's something about David—his presence feels comforting, almost like he carries a quiet strength within him. Though TJ has only just met him, David's gentle, accepting nature already feels like a safe place to land.

Tea Jay, still confused and afraid, tells Pastor David about the strange sensations he's been feeling since he arrived in the church.

"I believe this is God trying to convict your heart, Tea Jay. I think He wants you to give your life to God. May I pray for you?" David asks.

Embarrassed and overwhelmed by the growing attention, Tea Jay blushes. He's always had some belief in a higher power, but fear of ridicule kept him from admitting it.

"Yes, okay... What do I have to do?" Tea Jay asks hesitantly, unsure of what is happening to him.

"Are you willing to give your life to Jesus today?" David asks earnestly.

"I'll do anything to stop feeling like this. I just don't want to feel this way anymore," Tea Jay blurts out.

David asks again, with sincerity in his voice, "Are you ready to give your life to Christ?"

"I am, yes," Tea Jay replies, still somewhat confused but willing.

"We're going to pray the prayer of salvation now. Just repeat after me," David says.

Together, they pray: "I know I am a sinner and need your forgiveness. I believe you died in my place and rose from the grave to make me new and to prepare me to live in your presence forever. Jesus, come into my life, take control of my life, forgive my sins, and save me. I place my trust in You alone for my salvation, and I accept Your free gift of eternal life. Amen."

Although Tea Jay goes through the motions of the prayer, deep down he doesn't feel truly connected to it. He believes he's too far gone, too broken to be saved. His feelings of hopelessness weigh heavily on his heart.

Despite this, Tea Jay's core issue remains. He longs to feel loved and accepted but struggles with insecurity and a sense of unworthiness. The deep wounds of his past have left him unable to understand what true love is, and as a result, he mistakes lust for love, yearning for a connection that he believes he'll never have.

In his heart, Tea Jay still thinks: "Why would anyone else love me if my own family couldn't?"

His deep insecurity and fear have trapped him in a cycle of unhealthy relationships. He never learned how to receive love and, therefore, can't truly give it. He doesn't know what it feels like to be cared for, nurtured, or protected by a stable figure, so he can't break free from his emotional dependency on others. Every time he enters a relationship, he ends up lost in the need to feel validated, loved, and desired.

Time passes quickly, and soon, Tea Jay is due in court for sentencing. He knows he could face eighteen months to three years, or possibly even more. Frida urges him to attend court and face his consequences, but Tea Jay, consumed with fear and self-pity, decides not to go. He knows that a bench warrant will be issued for his arrest, but he convinces himself that he can still evade the inevitable.

Again, the weight of his actions presses down on him. He can't stop replaying the mistakes he's made, especially the fraud he committed in his uncle's name.

"Why the hell did I do that? My uncle was always good to me. What's wrong with me?" he torments himself, caught in a spiral of guilt and regret.

Consumed by fear of jail and the possibility of losing Frida, Tea Jay is desperate to avoid the inevitable.

Frida, unaware of the full extent of Tea Jay's trouble, invites him to stay at her mother's flat above their shop. Tea Jay eagerly accepts the offer, seeing it as a way to hide from the authorities. In his mind, he's convinced that as long as the police don't know about their relationship, they won't find him. He believes that without a fixed address and as long as he's not claiming benefits, he'll remain untraceable.

Tea Jay also knows that the police can only trace him through a benefit claim with the Department of Health and Social Security.

Tea Jay thinks he's clever by claiming no fixed abode and collecting his benefits from the social security office. He believes he's always a step ahead of the police, who are surely tracking his movements. His strategy is simple—keep switching his catchment area and transferring his case to different Department of Health and Social Security branches. Each time the paperwork catches up, he slips away to another district, confident he can buy a few more weeks.

The police are struggling to keep up with him. Tea Jay's slippery tactics and constant relocations leave them chasing paperwork, while Tea Jay takes full advantage of the delays in updating government records.

Tea Jay and Frida eventually move into a hostel together, a temporary haven where he keeps his benefits in her name to further avoid detection. But after nearly three months in the same place, Tea Jay starts to grow restless. The constant feeling of being hunted never fully fades, but as the weeks pass without any sign of the police, he becomes more complacent, telling himself, "Maybe they've forgotten about me."

Despite his relief at not being caught, Tea Jay's behaviour begins to spiral. He can't ignore the itch that drives him out of the hostel almost every night, seeking refuge in the bottle. Frida, now aware of his struggles with alcohol, starts to notice more troubling signs. Their relationship, once hopeful, is showing cracks. He's creating arguments for no reason, finding excuses to leave so he can drink. Even worse, money's disappearing from her cashpoint card, and small amounts of cash seem to go missing more frequently.

"Tea Jay, we need to talk," Frida says, her voice full of concern, as she faces him one evening. There's a sadness in her eyes that he can't brush off.

"What's going on? You want to finish with me, don't ya?" Tea Jay snaps back defensively, his voice rising as the paranoia seeps through his words. He's always prepared for abandonment, expecting it even before it happens.

WALKING THE LINE

I f Tea Jay is completely honest with himself, he knows deep down that he's unstable in many ways. He understands that anyone can father a child, but it takes someone truly special to be a dad. The thought of becoming a father splits him in two. On one hand, fear consumes him—he can barely take care of himself, let alone another life. But on the other hand, there's hope. If Frida is carrying his child, maybe this could be the turning point he so desperately needs.

Tea Jay drifts constantly into daydreams, craving to be liked, loved, and accepted—though often for all the wrong reasons. He imagines himself as a well-built, great-looking man with a tan that only those with wealth and status seem to have. In these fantasies, he's an executive, owning vast lands and properties purchased with winnings from the pools. Women are drawn to him, and his wife is stunning, falling over backward to keep him happy. His children worship him, looking up to him as a hero.

But in reality, Tea Jay is lost. His mind is filled with voices, mood swings, and the numbing haze of antipsychotic medication for his schizophrenia. His nights are plagued by relentless night terrors—flashes of childhood trauma, abuse, and the haunting memory of brutal attacks.

What he doesn't realize is that to be truly liked, loved, and accepted, it has to come from within.

The dream of becoming a balanced individual feels a lifetime away. To step into the role of a responsible father, Tea Jay first needs to face his past—he must confront the ghosts that have haunted him for so long and somehow find a way to forgive those who have hurt him.

There's a mountain of trauma from his childhood that he's never truly dealt with—years of mental, physical, and sexual abuse. They've left deep scars, but he's never learned how to heal.

For example, he can never forget the horrific attack in Bristol. The police had informed him they couldn't take the matter further—there wasn't enough evidence. It was his word against another's. That moment left him cold, feeling powerless. Without clear proof, justice wasn't possible. But until Tea Jay learns to confront his past without numbing the pain with alcohol, he knows deep down that he'll never truly find stability.

It's not just about facing his past. He needs to let go of the blame, the self-pity, and the desire to play the victim. Until he does, he'll remain broken, trapped in a cycle of irresponsibility. Without asking for help, he'll stay locked in an inebriated world of justification, always trying to control things but never really in control.

His thoughts are abruptly interrupted when Frida shakes him hard by the shoulder. She's furious—Tea Jay is drunk again. But behind her anger lies fear, her tears barely hidden behind a thin veil of hope. She stares at him with a look of melancholy, wondering if this man can ever be the father their child needs. All she longs for is for him to hold her, to take care of her, the way she has cared for him.

Frida is beautiful, her petite figure smartly dressed. She works as a beautician in her mother's salon. Standing at five feet two inches, her auburn hair falls just past her neck, framing her face, while her dark brown eyes, usually full of warmth, are now clouded with worry.

Frida is a few years younger than Tea Jay, and she's utterly besotted. She sees something kind and loving in him that others seem blind to.

But many people around her are quick to judge. They insist that unless Tea Jay stops drinking, she should end the relationship. They don't understand the illness he struggles with—how it warps the mind and ravages the body. They only see a man lost to narcissism, someone who pulls Frida into his destructive orbit. But Frida doesn't see it that way. All she wants is for people to give her partner a chance.

Frida tries to remind Tea Jay about their appointment for the pregnancy test at the doctor's tomorrow, but he's passed out beside an empty bottle of vodka and a half-empty bottle of Anadin. Her concern grows as she tries to wake him, but there's no response. Minutes pass, and finally, after several attempts, he stirs—only to lash out in fury at her, angry for simply reminding him about the day's plans.

Hours later, after they've both fallen asleep, Frida's panic returns. She wakes to find Tea Jay unresponsive, and she fears the worst. Believing he's not breathing; she frantically calls for an ambulance.

The paramedics arrive within minutes and rush Tea Jay to the hospital.

Moments later, Tea Jay finds himself sitting upright in the ambulance, feeling better than ever.

Confusion swirls in his mind. Why are they ignoring me? he wonders, calling out to the paramedics. He feels perfectly fine but doesn't understand why they can't hear him—or why they're ignoring him entirely.

A wave of hopelessness washes over him, dark and sinister, pulling him under. Suddenly, he's no longer in the ambulance. He's standing on an incredibly stormy, desolate island, surrounded by miles of black rocks and jagged mountains. He feels utterly worthless, frozen by the ice-cold wind.

Something deep within tells him that he's about to be judged for the sins he's committed—drug abuse, gluttony, dishonesty, and others that he's tried to bury.

In the distance, he hears a voice, friendly and warm, pleading with a higher force, as if asking for permission to intervene.

In an instant, Tea Jay is in a completely different place.

Warmth envelops him, and he finds himself sitting among a group of people in what seems like a small church. The church hall is oblong, with a long table in the centre, where people sit talking. Others sit by the walls, smiling and welcoming. They seem happy to see him, friendly even, but Tea Jay feels distant, like a closed book.

His attention is drawn to two sets of scrolls on the wall. The sight of them gives him a sense of peace, a strange comfort that begins to thaw the cold he felt earlier.

He tries to convince himself this is some wild dream. But something tells him otherwise.

Suddenly, he's no longer in the church. He finds himself in a doctor's office, though he doesn't know how he got there. His attention locks onto a green poster on the wall—a picture of someone trapped behind bars, locked in a bottle.

Tea Jay feels strangely calm, unafraid. A peaceful presence rests just to his left.

He senses something speaking to him—not with words, but telepathically. A sentence he saw years ago in a hospital in Bristol suddenly appears in his mind, clear as day:

"Tea Jay, you need to ask for help; I will help and do for you what you cannot do for yourself. Ask, and it shall be given."

Moments later, he feels an overwhelming presence—loving, peaceful, protective—holding him close. He's only ever felt this once before. Though the memory is faint, the sensation is familiar and comforting. Something powerful, filled with positive energy, surrounds him, filling him from within. The world around him brightens, and though he believes he must be dreaming, he pinches himself, trying to wake up.

Nevertheless, the words appear clearly in his mind:

"Tea Jay, pinching yourself won't work; you're here for a reason."

Suddenly, Tea Jay feels utterly powerless. He's sitting in a place of outer darkness, a bottle pressed to his lips. He looks lost, broken, drowning in oceans of fear and tears. Cupping his head in his hands, his heart shatters under the weight of it all.

"I need help," he mutters, feeling a deep, anguished emptiness. Yet, he's lost, with no memory of how he got here.

The word Pray! flashes in front of his eyes.

Moments later, a familiar prayer appears before him:

"Lord our God, I know I am a sinner, and I ask for your forgiveness. I believe you died for my sins and rose from the dead. I turn from my old ways and invite you into my heart and life. I want to trust and follow you as my Lord and Saviour. Amen!"

He cries out the prayer from deep within, and at that very moment, the warm, comforting presence surrounds him again, protective and filled with love.

Suddenly, Tea Jay finds himself in a completely different place.

His attention is drawn to something ahead of him, both familiar and strange. A figure stands before him—a man in a white robe, with feet that shine like polished bronze. Tea Jay can't place the man's origin; his face seems to shift, constantly changing.

Then a voice, like thunder, resounds around him:

"Do you know who I am, Tea Jay?"

"Jesus!" Tea Jay's mind answers, almost instinctively.

"Look at all these people as I open my sash, Tea Jay," the figure says.

As the sash is untied, Tea Jay sees what looks like thousands upon thousands of faces within the silhouette of the man's torso.

Whether Tea Jay looks left or right, the figure—who he believes in his soul to be the spirit of the universe—is always directly in front of him. The brilliant white floor beneath him stretches far and wide, with walls of the same radiant light on either side. Behind his higher power is the vast expanse of the universe, deep space unfolding endlessly.

Tea Jay feels an overwhelming rush of love and emotion as words form before his eyes:

"Every face you see here is part of my body, Tea Jay. My body is the church, and I want you to testify. Be one of my witnesses to all these people, and many more. No one comes to the Father except through me," Jesus says.

"Am I dead?" Tea Jay wonders, almost in disbelief.

At the very moment he questions his mortality, Tea Jay finds himself back in the ambulance, sitting upright.

The paramedics are calling his name.

"Tea Jay? Tea Jay? Code blue—he's flatlining again!"

Blissfully calm, Tea Jay watches the scene unfold, repeating softly to himself, "I'm fine. I'm okay. What's all the alarm?"

But the paramedics can't hear him. They frantically work on his lifeless body, trying to revive him, their voices growing more urgent.

Still, Tea Jay feels that same warm, protective presence just to his left.

In less than a second, an incredible force pulls him forward at lightning speed, propelling him through a bright, peaceful tunnel.

Suddenly, he's standing upright in the middle of a crystal-clear river. The water seems alive, welcoming him.

Ahead, he notices a figure sitting on a massive, majestic throne. The figure's face is brighter than a thousand suns, impossible to see clearly. A powerful waterfall—made of living water—flows from the figure's torso, gushing toward Tea Jay, through him, and around him. Yet, the water doesn't feel wet. Instead, it feels alive, loving, and profoundly welcoming.

In the next moment, Tea Jay is handed a heavy bag, packed full of change. A deep sense of depression washes over him as the words twenty and five years appear in front of his eyes, though he has no idea what they mean.

His thoughts are crowded, one pushing out the next, leaving him unable to focus.

Then, without warning, an icy-cold fear grips him. The darkness deepens, and dread fills his entire psyche. The face of a tarot card reader suddenly appears before him.

Moments later, the word Lies... flashes before his eyes.

The word pierces him, cutting deep into his soul like a red-hot knife through butter.

He feels the fear intensify. Something inside him warns that unless he renounces these lies, he could be in grave spiritual danger.

A deep conviction settles in—he knows many parts of his life need to change, drastically.

Although Tea Jay can feel the spirit communicating with him, it's as if another spirit is speaking through him. Suddenly, Tea Jay senses he's not quite himself. He feels positive, but strangely different.

"Tea Jay, I will only ever do for you what you are unable to do for yourself. I'm going to renew a steadfast spirit within you, but you'll suffer the consequences of your actions. When you return to your life, you'll go to prison for your crimes. You'll always have a choice, Tea Jay. It's up to you to make the right one." The spirits voice echoes with finality.

In a split second, Tea Jay finds himself standing beside Frida at home. She greets him with a smile and a loving kiss. Startled, Tea Jay feels undeserving of her affection, confused, as if trying to remember something important.

Moments later, he brushes the confusion aside, accepting her love as if it were the most normal thing in the world. There's a strong sense of love, positivity, and ease between them. But deep down, Tea Jay remains confused, almost as if searching for a reason why Frida shouldn't trust him.

"We've got to go to the hospital to see Joseph later, Tea Jay," Frida says, worry evident in her voice.

Just as Tea Jay is about to ask, Who's Joseph? he's suddenly transported. In an instant, he's standing inside what appears to be a prison cell.

He's behind a prisoner who is praying, though Tea Jay can't see the man's face. The prisoner seems unaware of Tea Jay's presence, yet occasionally looks around, sensing something. Outside the cell, in the exercise yard, Tea Jay sees two men—danger lurking in their intentions. He senses the threat but has no way of warning the praying man not to go outside.

Moments later, Tea Jay finds himself looking down as if from a ceiling. Below him, in a hospital prison cell, one prisoner smiles at another, a man wearing a bright crucifix that glows luminously.

Then, just as abruptly, Tea Jay is in an operating theatre. Surgeons move around the table, but instead of a patient, they are cutting open what seems to be a bag of sugar.

Suddenly, Tea Jay is standing in space, the Earth just below him to his left. In front of him is a queue of people, though they have no solid form. They appear as faint silhouettes of cloudy mist.

Before he realizes it, Tea Jay is at the front of the line, and he hears an incredibly resounding voice speak.

"It's time to return to your life, Tea Jay. I'm going to send you my book. I want you to read and study it. You'll know it's from me when you receive it because you'll feel it."

Tea Jay asks, "I need help with so many things. Please help me stop drinking and smoking."

"I will always do for you that you cannot do for yourself. However, I won't do for you what you are capable of doing for yourself," the voice replies.

A moment later, Tea Jay wakes up in a hospital bed, thinking he's at home. His first instinct is to call out for Frida.

"Frida, I just had the craziest, messed-up dream."

But before he can process it, something beyond his control pulls him back to sleep. Within moments, he's back in space, the globe floating just below his feet. The same thunderous voice fills the void around him.

"It wasn't a dream, Tea Jay. When you wake, you won't remember what's happened or what you've been shown. You will receive a blessing, though to others, it may appear as an illness. This will be the way I communicate with you. You will remember my words, but the events themselves will come back to you only after they've occurred. This is because you're not meant to know your destiny."

Tea Jay wakes up again, this time with wires from a heart monitor attached to his chest.

"How long have I been in here?" he asks weakly, his voice hoarse.

The doctor, taking his pulse, looks at him intently. "A few days. You're very lucky to be alive. Your heart stopped three times—twice on the way to the hospital and once more a few hours ago."

A wave of fear passes through Tea Jay as he's haunted by a familiar, terrifying memory from his last out-of-body experience in Bristol.

A few days after being discharged, Tea Jay and Frida sit nervously in the doctor's office, waiting for the pregnancy results.

When the doctor finally calls them in, they sit together, filled with tension.

"Well, Frida, you're at least ten weeks pregnant," the doctor says with a smile.

"Shit," Tea Jay mutters to himself, clutching Frida's hand tightly.

Within a couple of months, Tea Jay and Frida find a flat in the Midlands, and Tea Jay secures a job as a care assistant. But a month later, he loses the job after being caught fiddling his hours on the rota. He quickly lands another job at a petrol station, but that, too, lasts only a few weeks before his drinking costs him the position.

Two days later, desperate, Tea Jay and Frida make a joint claim and head to the Department of Health & Social Security for a crisis loan.

It's April, and the cold bites as they enter the DHSS building. They face four steep flights of stairs—there are no lifts. Frida, now twenty-six weeks pregnant, has to stop and sit down, wincing from a sharp pain in her stomach.

At the top of the stairs, they enter a crowded waiting area filled with rowdy, impatient people shouting at the staff. The seats are cold, uncomfortable metal, and they wait for hours as tempers flare around them.

Suddenly, Frida cries out to Tea Jay, her voice panicked. "My waters have broken!"

Panic floods Tea Jay, and he shouts at the staff to call an ambulance.

The staff eye him with suspicion, assuming he's lying to get quicker service. But when they see the growing pool of water at Frida's feet, her screams filling the room, they spring into action.

Without hesitation, the now-urgent staff rush to her side and immediately call for an ambulance.

A BAG OF SUGAR

Trapped in a prison of his own making, Tea Jay shakes violently from the lack of booze. His mind is fogged, unable to think straight. He's confined within an icy vortex of powerlessness and unmanageability, spiralling further and further away from his true self.

Here stands a twenty-four-year-old child locked in a man's body, drowning in his own misery, wondering what's next.

Warnings ring in his head, but he ignores them. He doesn't know how to fight the obsession with alcohol, so his mind clings to the lie that keeps feeding him more lies.

"Fuck everything and run! Take a drink; don't take a drink. Ahh, fuck it!"

The sweet nectar slides down his throat, bringing a fleeting sense of warmth and comfort, followed by the familiar feeling of ahh, thank fuck for that.

Bliss flows through him as his mind slips into a blackout.

Hours later, at the hospital, Tea Jay sways back and forth as the midwife informs Frida that she has an infection in the placenta, causing her to go into labour three months early.

"What must be going through this poor woman's mind?" the mid-wife wonders. "What kind of man calls himself her partner, the father of her child, and shows up wasted? What kind of life will this baby have, if he even survives?"

Hours pass, and Frida gives birth to a tiny baby boy, weighing just one pound fourteen ounces. There are life-threatening complications, and the nurse rushes the newborn to the neonatal intensive care unit.

A few hours later, Frida lies on the ward, her mother by her side.

"Where have they taken my grandson?" Frida's mom asks the mid-wife.

"Please try not to worry. We've taken him to be monitored and placed in an incubator because he's so small," the midwife replies, her worry seeping through her calm tone.

"Have you thought of a name?" Frida's mom asks gently.

"Well, I'm definitely not naming him after his dad," Frida cries, her voice thick with frustration and sadness.

"That bastard Tea Jay! I won't let him wreck my daughter's and grandson's lives. Why can't he just stop drinking, for their sake if not his own?" Frida's mom fumes silently.

"I hope my son doesn't turn out to be a bloody boozer like his father," Frida thinks, worry etched deep in her heart.

A couple of hours later, Tea Jay begins to sober up, both he and Frida looking deeply concerned as they learn their son has a swollen stomach and isn't feeding properly. He's also vomiting green bile and constipated. The doctor informs them that the baby has Necrotising Enterocolitis (N.E.C.), a serious condition that affects newborns by inflaming the tissue in the intestines.

"Maybe God is using my sick son to get my attention, to make me stop drinking. But I can't stop for anyone, not even my own son," Tea Jay thinks, trapped in his addiction.

"Don't worry, babe. I won't drink heavily again, I promise," Tea Jay slurs, unsteady on his feet.

"Promises, promises. I've heard it all before, Tea Jay. You've got a son now and a woman who loves you. We need to think of a name. What are we going to call him?" Frida asks, her voice tinged with exhaustion.

"Funny you should mention that. I had the name Joseph in my head just before you asked. I'm having déjà vu again. I swear I know that name from somewhere, but I can't remember where," Tea Jay says, looking upward, trying to search his foggy memory.

"Funny you should mention Joseph. You asked me who Joseph was six months ago in the hospital when your heart stopped. You were telling me about a vivid dream you had, but then your heart stopped again before you could finish," Frida says.

"Did I? I don't remember. But Joseph is a lovely name—it's biblical," Tea Jay says.

The neonatal unit rushes little Joseph to the children's hospital in Birmingham for a laparotomy to remove part of his intestine.

On the day of the operation, the parents sit anxiously in the doctor's office as the doctor explains that Joseph has a 50/50 chance of survival.

"For fuck's sake, I need a drink. Just one to calm my nerves. Frida won't mind; she'll understand," Tea Jay tells himself, succumbing to the lie again.

A day or two later, Joseph's condition worsens; he still isn't feeding properly. The parents are called back into the office. Although the surgery was somewhat successful, Joseph now needs another operation to insert feeding tubes through his neck and into his intestines.

While Frida worries, Tea Jay is too drunk most of the time to think clearly, let alone care.

Frida's faith in God keeps her going, trusting that He wouldn't bring Joseph into the world only to take him away so soon. But the rest of the family fears the worst. Despite everything, Tea Jay stays by his son's side, holding his tiny hand through the incubator's opening.

Joseph's hand is barely the size of two fingernails.

Joseph is tiny, born at just 1 pound 14 and a half ounces—so small he fits in the palm of a hand like a bag of sugar. The doctors didn't expect him to survive, but TJ feels something deeper, something unshakable. God whispers to his heart that Joseph will pull through. Yet, even as his son battles for life, TJ is lost in his own world, too distracted by his own struggles, looking at everything else but the reality in front of him. Joseph undergoes five or six major operations, each one a miracle in itself. He's TJ's little miracle baby, but in that moment, TJ can't see the wake-up call. It's still all about him, and he's not ready to listen.

Weeks later, Frida and Tea Jay return for more news. The doctors inform them that Joseph may have liver damage due to being born so prematurely, but they are optimistic that it is treatable.

Two weeks pass, and Joseph's health appears to improve. But then, the doctors rush him into surgery again, this time to tie two open valves in his heart that carry blood to the upper chambers.

David McNeil, the pastor at Frida and Tea Jay's church, along with the church community and both families, pray fervently for Joseph's recovery. Despite his drinking, Tea Jay remains strong in his faith that God will heal his son. A month later, with Joseph still struggling, the pastor dedicates him to the Lord.

Three months later, Joseph begins to improve significantly. Frida and Tea Jay reach out to the Evening Mail to share their story, hoping to inspire other parents of premature babies.

A week after their story appears in both The Daily and Evening Mail, Central News requests an interview, dubbing Joseph the "Child of Hope" in 1995.

A month later, Joseph is discharged and finally allowed to go home.

"How the hell am I supposed to cope with a kid? I can't even take care of myself, let alone Frida and my son. I'm in debt up to my eyeballs, wanted by the police, not working, and to top it off, I bet God hates me for going through all this shit. Ahh, fuck it, I need a drink," Tea Jay thinks, feeling the familiar pull of his addiction.

Two months later, just after collecting his benefits, Tea Jay hears a loud knock at the door.

Frida answers, her eyes clouding with sudden darkness.

"What's wrong, babe?" Tea Jay asks, puffing on a cigarette and taking a swig of Stella.

"It's for you, Tea Jay," she says, her voice heavy with concern.

As Tea Jay walks to the door, a face he'd rather not see steps into the living room.

"Oh, fuck no!" Tea Jay thinks as the police officer strides in.

"You knew this was coming, Tea. We'd catch up with you sooner or later. You can't walk away from this. You've got a bench warrant out for your arrest at crown court for sentencing. Funny thing is, we forgot about you for a while, but when we saw your story in the news, we said, 'Oh yes, Tea Jay.'"

The officer pauses, then adds, "I'm arresting you for failure to appear at crown court. You didn't think this would just go away, did you? You might get a suspended sentence or probation given your son's situation. Who knows?"

"Can I say goodbye to my son and wife, and have a quick smoke before we leave?" Tea Jay asks.

"Of course. So, this is the miracle baby, huh? I'll give you a minute to say your goodbyes," the officer says, surprisingly understanding.

CUSTODY BATTLE

Although Tea Jay manages to turn around long enough to look out of the rear window from the back seat of the unmarked police car, he's not quick enough to notice Frida standing outside, tears streaming down her face, holding their son. She watches as her partner is led away, her mind racing.

"How am I going to cope without Tea Jay to help me with Joseph? I can't cope on my own," Frida thinks desperately.

Tea Jay, on the other hand, can only think of locking Frida, Joseph, and the image of their home into his memory, fearing the looming prison sentence. His stomach churns with the awful uncertainty of whether Frida will wait for him. Deep down, he knows he doesn't deserve her. He's betrayed her in so many ways—slept around, stolen from her, insulted her, even struck her. He's left her alone for days on end without food or money, always putting his first love—alcohol—before her and their child.

"I'll be back in ten minutes," Tea Jay would lie. "Just popping up to the shop to get some fags." But those ten minutes often turned into days, as he lost himself in drugs and booze.

Now, the weight of his actions comes crashing down like a thunderbolt. The full gravity of his situation hits him hard, and his heart sinks with the realization that he's the architect of his own misery.

"She's gone. I've lost her. She won't wait. I'm nothing but a pisshead and a fuckin' loser," the voices scream in his head, causing it to pound.

Tears stream down Tea Jay's face, each one feeling like it's burning his skin. Finally, he starts to grasp the magnitude of his actions and the inevitable consequences.

"Get a grip. You're only crying because you got caught. You never had any intention of handing yourself in," a voice within mocks him.

As he sits in the back of the police car, driven toward the Crown Court, regret gnaws at his insides. He realizes, far too late, the depth of his partner's despair—Frida, who's barely getting by with enough money to feed herself and their child.

Regret after regret crashes over him, a tidal wave of guilt and self-loathing. "I need to change my bastard ways. Idiot! My family needs me. I'm 25 years old. Grow up, you prat," Tea Jay mutters to himself, pacing anxiously in his cell before court.

"You're only sorry because you got caught. You wouldn't change otherwise, you're just a pisshead," the voice in his head echoes relentlessly.

Then, a sudden thought interrupts everything else.

"You need to ask for help, Tea Jay," a voice screams from deep within his spirit.

But almost immediately, another voice counters, "You're only sorry because you got caught. You'll never change."

"What the fuck?" Tea Jay mutters to himself. "Wait a minute... you need to ask for help?" he says, déjà vu overwhelming him. He frantically searches his memory, trying to make sense of the repeating pattern.

In the meantime, Tea Jay gives his barrister, Mr. Phillips, his final instructions, silently screaming in his mind for bail.

It's all about him now. He doesn't care about anyone or anything, only about escaping remand. He feeds his barrister sob story after sob story, manipulating every angle, desperate to avoid custody. Deep down, though, it's not just about losing Frida that scares him. What truly terrifies him is being locked up and forced to face the demons that haunt him—his own insecurities and the child he sees in the mirror.

As Tea Jay is led from his tiny, Spartan holding cell under the Crown Court, he's taken up cold, steep concrete steps that lead into the courtroom. The weight of doom hangs in the air, thick and oppressive. There's no escape behind the reinforced bulletproof glass that surrounds him. This is where he'll meet his fate.

Mr. Phillips mitigates the circumstances to the Recorder-Judge, addressing the original breach of bail.

"The first issue, Your Honour, is the pregnancy of the defendant's partner," Phillips begins.

"And secondly, it was the premature birth of their very poorly son that prevented Mr. Jay from handing himself in earlier," he adds.

But Tea Jay knows the truth—he's just spinning lies, manipulating the situation because he's terrified of encountering a certain enemy already inside the prison. No way is he admitting that, though—not to the court, not to his brief.

Phillips makes two applications to the Crown: one for an adjournment of sentencing, and the second for conditional bail.

Tea Jay continues to manipulate, convincing Phillips to request a long list of bail conditions—signing at the police station, residence requirements, the works.

The judge, however, remains unfazed.

"I'm willing to grant one of the requests, Mr. Phillips. I will adjourn sentencing for six weeks," the Recorder-Judge says. "But your client, Mr. Jay, has no chance of receiving bail. His breaches of bail conditions are far too numerous, and he's been at large for twelve months. Bail denied."

Then, turning to Tea Jay, the judge says with a finality that chills the air, "Stand up, Mr. Jay. You are remanded in custody until sentencing."

In the cells under the court, Tea Jay asks the prison officer, "What nick am I going to, gov?"

"Winson Green," the officer replies.

"For fuck's sake, shit!" Tea Jay mutters, his heart sinking even further.

"What's the matter?" the officer inquires.

"There's an arch-enemy in there, gov," Tea Jay confesses, panic settling in.

"Who is it? Why's he after you?" the officer asks.

"It doesn't matter, gov," Tea Jay sighs, unwilling to say more.

"Well, that's the consequence of committing crimes," the officer thinks silently. "If there's any bother, just let us know," the officer says aloud.

Tea Jay scoffs. "Yeah, yeah, whatever, gov."

Inside his mind, Tea Jay's panic continues to swirl. "Fuck, I'm dead!" he thinks, fear gripping his chest as the prison van transports him to Winson Green. The small cell inside the van feels like it's closing in on him.

His heart races faster and faster, panic rising to the surface. Frida's face flashes in his mind for just a second, making his stomach lurch.

Once at the prison gates, Tea Jay composes himself. He knows from experience that any sign of fear is seen as weakness in jail. And weakness gets you killed. He steps out of the van and switches into jail mentality—leave everything from the outside behind. Trust no one. Borrow nothing. Always look over your shoulder. Don't snitch.

After hours of waiting in the holding cell, Tea Jay is strip-searched and examined by the prison doctor.

"I feel suicidal," Tea Jay lies to the doctor, trying to avoid being sent to A-Wing where his enemy awaits.

The plan works. He's sent to the hospital wing instead.

The overpowering smell of cleaning fluids and carbolic soap fills the reception area, but as Tea Jay is briefly walked through the general population on the way to the hospital wing, the familiar scent of Old Holborn tobacco cuts through everything else.

Once there, Tea Jay is placed in a single cell under constant surveillance, told to strip off and put on a horrible brown plastic suit—a t-shirt and shorts. It's cold and degrading.

The next few days pass in isolation. Tea Jay constantly feels as if he's been here before. Déjà vu grips him tightly.

He knows he's never been on this wing before. So why does everything feel so familiar?

All he hears, day in and day out, is the endless clanging of doors and keys.

It's during one of these monotonous moments that Tea Jay recalls and recites a poem a former cellmate once wrote on the prison walls.

DOORS & KEYS

Keys And Doors, Doors and Keys
Stark White Walls, Doors and Keys
Echoes Abound but Don't Appease

Bars On the Windows Doors and Keys

All of Life's Lessons Come to Nought
It Wasn't My Fault but Still I Got Caught
All Satan's Work but They Blame Him for Nought
How Can It Be It Was Only a Thought

Got to Be Strong Got to Be Tough
Got To Swear Is It Enough
Show Of My Tattoos Shave of My Hair
But Under the Mask the Pain Is Laid Bare

Oh, Hear Me Sweet Jesus, Hear Me as I Pray
Open Their Eyes Lord Let Their Pain Go Away
Break Satan's strong Hold and Let Them Be Free
Never Again to Hear a Door and A Key

A friendly prisoner with a Scouse accent, one of the cleaners, opens
Tea Jay's hatch.

"Hello, mate. What you in for?" the prisoner asks.

"Fraud! Who're you?" Tea Jay responds.

"I'm one of the lifers. Call me Scouse. I'm one of the cleaners,"
Scouse says.

After a couple of days, Tea Jay realizes he's sharing the wing
with some notorious criminals—men who've committed unspeakable
crimes, including horrible murders.

Tea Jay connects with Scouse and another lifer, also a cleaner.
He feels somewhat protected, knowing that both men are not only
friendly but also happen to be Christians.

One morning, while Scouse is talking to him through the hatch, Tea Jay suddenly looks around and up at the ceiling. He senses something, or someone, behind him—a warm, familiar feeling.

"What are you looking at, mate?" Scouse asks, noticing Tea Jay's gaze toward the light. Still, nothing is there.

"Nothing, just a feeling of déjà vu. It's like I've been here before... but I haven't."

The next day, Scouse hands Tea Jay a New Living Translation Bible. As Tea Jay holds it, he feels a sensation of warmth and protection all around him. As Scouse speaks through the hatch, Tea Jay glances up at the corner of his cell again, feeling the same presence, though no one is there.

"Poor guy's obviously having the DTs and hallucinations from coming off the ale," Scouse thinks to himself.

Tea Jay becomes concerned about these bouts of déjà vu and puts in an application to see the doctor on the wing. However, when he speaks to one of the male nurses, the nurse just laughs.

"Get a grip, mate. It's just déjà vu—nothing serious. Stop wasting our time," the nurse says dismissively.

A couple of weeks later, Tea Jay is told to pack his kit—he's being moved to A-Wing.

Tea Jay panics. Even though "Rule 43" is the last place he wants to go—filled with nonces and all sorts of vile scum—he swallows his pride and requests a move to the protection wing, believing a certain acquaintance wants to kill him on A-Wing.

"Why's this guy after you, Jay?" the officer asks.

"I've done something I regret... but it's too late for that now," Tea Jay admits.

"Well, sorry to say, there's no room on the protection wing. You're heading to A-Wing, so pack your kit."

Tea Jay's heart races and his stomach somersaults as he walks through C-Wing from healthcare toward the centre. As he approaches A-Wing, a familiar face sneers at him.

"Just the fuckin' man. Watch what's going to happen—it will, when you least expect it," goes through his enemy's mind.

"Fuckin' hell, Jay. You've put on some timber. How long you doing?" Paca says, amused.

"Remanded for sentence," Tea Jay replies, nervous.

A couple of weeks later, Tea Jay's cellmate advises him to write a letter to the judge before sentencing, telling him it could work in his favour.

Six weeks later, the day before sentencing, Tea Jay writes the letter.

The judge, upon receiving the letter, addresses Tea Jay in court.

"Mr. Jay, I believe what you said in your letter—that you regret your actions against your uncle and that you want to change, to seek help for your alcoholism. Therefore, when you are eventually released, I hope you implement these changes into your life as you've promised. I'm going to give you the minimum sentence I'd originally planned.

Mr. Jay, I'm sentencing you to fifteen months in prison. Take him down," the judge declares.

Tea Jay feels conflicted. If he's honest with himself, he wrote the letter out of fear, trying to manipulate the judge into feeling sorry for his situation and hoping for probation instead.

As Christmas 1995 approaches, Tea Jay has about four months left to serve. He's been moved to K-Wing, hoping to get away from his enemy, but Paca has followed and ended up on the same wing.

Despite this, Tea Jay is doing well. He's getting on with a lot of the other prisoners and has become a model inmate. One week, before receiving a letter from a Bible company apologizing for being out of stock, Tea Jay unexpectedly receives a Bible in the post. As he looks at it, Tea Jay feels something alive, a living emotion penetrating his psyche. He experiences another bout of déjà vu—stronger this time—and feels a familiar warmth, as though something is communicating with him.

He has an epiphany, a profound realization, followed by yet another déjà vu—a memory of once was, but with more depth and meaning.

"I'm going to send you my book, Tea Jay. When you receive it, I want you to study it," echoes through Tea Jay's mind as a loving emotion, alive and flowing, surrounds his heart.

"Where have I heard that before?" Tea Jay wonders aloud, feeling something loving and protective hold him.

Tea Jay's cell is on the 1st floor, in the far-right corner of K-Wing, facing the B-Wing exercise yard. One day, he receives a note through his door.

"It's canteen tomorrow, and I want all your canteen. Again. Remember, if you don't, I'll tell everyone you're a grass," his enemy writes.

Tea Jay hits the buzzer and tells the officer he's being bullied, asking for a move.

The officer reassures Tea Jay, "Don't worry. Paca's got a shock coming his way. You'll be fine."

If Tea Jay is completely honest, he knows in his heart that he owes Paca more than money could ever repay. After all, it was Paca who introduced him to Frida the last time he was on remand.

Exercise is called! Nevertheless, something within tells Tea Jay to stay in his cell.

"Tea Jay, come outside, my friend! I'm not going to touch you; that stuff's been dealt with," Paca shouts through Tea Jay's cell window from the exercise yard.

"You know what needs to be done when he comes out on the exercise yard. There's hardly any screws about, and besides, they're busy over there in the corner anyway," Paca whispers to another con.

Paca stands with another prisoner, one who looks menacing, and again, something tells Tea Jay not to go outside.

Another epiphany strikes him—a déjà vu. A sudden wave of intense fear washes over him. He begins to pray inwardly, sensing someone behind him. He turns, but no one is there—only the cold emptiness of his cell.

The next day, Tea Jay submits an application to see the doctor.

His application is approved, and he explains to the doctor—who happens to be a psychiatrist—that he's been experiencing sudden bouts of déjà vu. Immediately, the doctor requests that Tea Jay be transferred to the hospital wing for assessment and to undergo an Electroencephalography (EEG).

Six weeks later, Tea Jay is informed that he may have Temporal Lobe Epilepsy. He is told that when he's released from custody, he'll need to see a specialist, and will likely undergo a CT scan to determine if epilepsy is the root cause.

Within moments, Tea Jay experiences yet another déjà vu, accompanied by a sudden memory.

The words, "You're going to receive a blessing, Tea Jay. However, to those in life, it will appear as an illness. But this is how it should be, as it's the way I'll communicate with you," echo in his mind.

He feels an overwhelming emotion—loving and protective—flooding his heart. It engulfs him, flowing within and throughout his being.

Four months later, Tea Jay is released from custody.

"You seem distant, Tea Jay. Aren't you glad to see me?" Frida asks, looking concerned.

"Yeah, course!" Tea Jay responds with a huff.

"Why did I even get Frida to meet me at the prison gate? I just want a couple of beers to celebrate getting out. There's no way that's happening with her breathing over my shoulder," Tea Jay thinks to himself.

He's been told that if he ever drinks again, it could kill him—especially if he consumes the quantities he used to. Adding to the danger is his epilepsy, which requires strong medication that could be fatal if mixed with alcohol.

Though Frida is impressed with Tea Jay for keeping his word and staying off alcohol and cigarettes for a while, she starts to notice the return of some of his old negative and selfish behaviours. Nevertheless, to both Frida and Tea Jay, alcohol remains the perceived core issue.

Still, Frida notices that Tea Jay's moods are beginning to resurface again.

One morning, Tea Jay has a spiritual experience as he realizes Frida has left £30 on her dresser, as well as her bag and purse in the living room. He feels honoured that she trusts him again, believing he has changed his manipulative ways. Yet, the unresolved issues from his past continue to haunt him, making them hard to cope with.

"Pastor Dave's at the door!" Frida shouts to Tea Jay, who's busy fighting his way through a jungle of reeds and unkempt grass in the back garden.

Dave is greeted by the mouth-watering aroma of mint sauce mixed with beef gravy from the Sunday roast.

"Hi, Tea Jay. You look lost in all that grass—need a hand?" Dave asks, noticing the state of the garden.

Dave is about five feet nine inches tall, with warm, welcoming dark brown eyes and neck-length hair. He has a light brown complexion and a slim-to-medium build, with a stylish sense of dress.

As Dave enters the modest two-bedroom ground floor flat, he steps directly into the living room from the front door. Directly ahead is Joseph's small bedroom, with the master bedroom immediately to the right. The living room walls are a warm peach colour, with a rustic pine coffee table in the centre of the room. To the left is a three-seater dark brown leather sofa, facing a large television, with a matching two-seater against the adjacent wall.

"Would you like a coffee, Dave?" Frida asks, juggling several tasks at once, including dinner preparations.

"Ooh, yes, please. Just one sugar and milk," Dave replies as he sits down.

"Dinner won't be long, guys. Tea Jay, come wash your hands," Frida calls out, noticing Tea Jay's muddy condition.

"You aren't coming into this house with those boots! Take them outside and knock the mud off them. Come on, hurry up, dinner's ready," Frida frowns at him.

"Stop whining, you silly mare!" Tea Jay jokes, laughing at her.

"Can I ask you a personal question, Tea Jay?" Dave inquires.

"Fire away!" Tea Jay responds, opening his arms in a welcoming gesture.

"What was it like in prison?" Dave asks, his curiosity getting the better of him.

Tea Jay frowns and shakes his head in disbelief at the question.

"Absolutely amazing; I loved every minute of it," Tea Jay mutters sarcastically under his breath.

Nevertheless, before Tea Jay can continue, Frida jumps in...

"Oh my gosh, now I've gone and put my foot in it; I hope I've not offended Tea Jay & Frida," Dave thinks to himself.

"Tea Jay, he's only asking."

"Well, what sort of bleeding question's that? Sorry I barked at you, Dave. It's just I don't want to be reminded about sodding prison." As Tea Jay attempts to finish his sentence, the pastor goes on to say...

"I totally understand where you're coming from, Tea Jay. Nevertheless, I just wanted to try and understand what you must have felt and experienced whilst in prison. I also need to know if you're ready for baptism, considering you're being baptized next Sunday," the pastor gently asks.

"Okay, Dave, I'll tell you exactly what it's like. The day I was locked up, as the unmarked police car drove up the road where we live, my stomach sunk.

For a brief moment, I managed to look around out the rear window of the car, just enough to lock my home, Mrs., and son into my memory.

I was screaming silently within in tears of dread and desperation.

I was lost and very afraid. Deep down, what hope of bail I had was shattered by my past deeds. I was desperate, I was alone, and had absolutely nowhere to turn except to face the consequences of four unwelcoming walls that screamed nothing but...

Think.

Think.

Think.

My life was in the hands of my consequences. I was to face the hideous four horsemen of terror, bewilderment, frustration, and complete and utter despair.

I was lost in a never-ending black portal of what next.

As I was remanded in custody, leaving the Crown Court, my inner hope was that the prison van would take hours to reach the Green, simply because the fear of what, who, and when enveloped me. Nevertheless, my hope of a long journey was shattered fifteen minutes later as the sweat-box entered the prison gate.

Leaving the prison van "sweat-box," I was told to take a seat with about seven other cons in reception. A load of bad eggs thrown together in one basket, so to speak.

Being dehumanized, I was stripped of my only identity. My clothes and personal effects were stored, and I wouldn't see them again until sentencing and then the eventual day of my release.

I was asked very intrusive personal questions, I had a thorough strip search, and a very thorough medical. Then I was made to wait for hours in a holding cell.

In jail, you have to be on guard at all times and need to be constantly looking over your shoulder. You can't show any fear whatsoever or you'll become someone's bitch.

Years passed, in and out of prison, I've often thought to myself. That's it now! I'm going straight, no more drinking, no more fraud, no more pain. I need to change my ways.

Prison's not the solution because it can't fix the problem; it's just a health resort for the liver.

You go in one door and come out the same one when released.

However, the off-licence or boozer's just round the corner.

Prison can't keep me sober! So, what's the solution, Dave?" Tea Jay asks, looking bemused.

"God can help!" Dave says gently.

"Really, Dave; how?" Tea Jay asks, looking down.

"Ask him for help, Tea Jay," Dave says softly.

"I'm not an alcoholic, Dave," Tea Jay says with a look of melancholy.

"Who mentioned anything about being an alcoholic? I certainly haven't, Tea Jay. Do you think God might be talking directly to your heart? Just keep an open mind," Dave comments.

Tea Jay starts to become teary-eyed. Nevertheless, he manages to snap out of it quickly as he doesn't want to show any kind of weakness. He doesn't admit that sometimes he struggles with accepting his past and generally uses this as one of many excuses to take a drink.

"Just give me a sec, I need to get some tissue because I've got dry eyes, Dave," Tea Jay says as he hopes the pastor doesn't clock a tear he sheds.

"Are you okay, Tea Jay?" Frida asks as she puts her arms around him.

"Yeah, of course, I am," Tea Jay says, going red.

"Ooh, since when have you suffered from dry eyes? If you're struggling, you need to drop the macho rubbish and actually ask for help, Tea Jay. This is our pastor and one of the reasons he's here," Frida mentions.

"I can't believe him and personally believe God's trying to communicate and trying to tell Tea Jay to ask for help. God will only do for him that he can't do for himself; he won't do for him what Tea can do for himself," a very frustrated Frida thinks to herself.

Tea Jay manages to convince both his partner and Dave that he's okay and reminds Frida that the pastor predominantly came to their home to talk through the baptism. Nevertheless, Dave goes on to say.

"I know I've come here with the view to talking to you both about your baptism, Tea Jay. However, it's also my job to care for God's flock, especially within Sutton Coldfield Vineyard. Being ready for baptism is all about being ready for change, or if you prefer ready to accept help when needed," the pastor states.

Two weeks later, just after the baptism, Tea Jay decides to test the waters with Frida.

"Shall we celebrate with just one drink?"

Frida frowns, visibly upset, reminding him that his baptism is meant to signify a new beginning. As she speaks, she catches a familiar scent.

"Have you been smoking, Tea Jay? Don't lie to me, I'm warning you!" she snaps.

"For crying out loud, will you quit nagging? No, I haven't smoked. Even if I did, that's not the problem, is it? I'm getting fed up with your constant fussing."

"By the way, who was that guy on the phone earlier? He seems a bit too friendly for just a customer at the salon," Tea Jay says, suspicion creeping in.

"He's a friend I've known for ages; I mentioned him when I visited you in prison," Frida replies, looking anxious.

"Then why were you whispering?" Tea Jay challenges.

"What is wrong with me? Why does my head feel like it's on fire? I'm trying to stay sober, I've given up drinking, and I'm paying the bills, yet I still feel terrible about myself."

"Maybe it's not just the drinking," Tea Jay thinks, grappling with his thoughts.

Over the next couple of months, Frida notices Tea Jay becoming more irritable, snapping at the smallest things.

"I need a smoke; I'm going to buy some fags," he declares.

"No, you're not, Tea Jay! You promised to quit. If you start drinking again, I will leave and take Joseph with me," Frida shouts back.

"Oh, whatever, Frida! I'm not going to drink; I just need a cigarette to calm my nerves, alright?"

As he steps out of the flat, a grin spreads across his face as he reflects, "Thank goodness I'm away from her constant nagging. I just need something to ease my nerves. A few cans of lager won't hurt; I'm not an alcoholic since I've stayed sober for twelve months on my own. A few drinks won't matter; she'll understand."

Entering the off-licence to buy cigarettes, he hears a familiar voice. It feels like an old friend, filled with warmth and excitement, whispering, "You can drink like a gentleman and then stop; you'll be fine. You're not an alcoholic. You've been sober for a year; you're cured. If you were really an alcoholic, you'd have drunk that hooch your cellmate brewed in jail. Go on, Frida will understand."

Tea Jay hesitates, staring at the brandy and packs of Stella, lost in thought as the shop assistant grows impatient. He feels a mix of nervous excitement and the allure of something familiar.

"What can I get you?" the assistant asks.

THE MIRROR

It's a blistering hot sunny day, and as Tea Jay perspires heavily, he tries to think up a tall story to convince his girlfriend that, this time, it actually wasn't his fault.

Instead of undoing his shirt, he rips the buttons off his beer-stained top. Suddenly coming to his senses, he has a brief moment of clarity as he thinks to himself:

"Oh fuck, she'll freak; why do I get myself into this shit? I need help!"

As he staggers down the road where he lives, days after telling Frida he was just popping to the shop for cigarettes, he can't help but notice one of his neighbour's smiling at him. He blushes, then suddenly belches at the attractive young lady who's caught his attention.

"Hello, what's your name?" the slim brunette asks, as Tea Jay smiles with lustful eyes.

"Depends," Tea Jay flirts as he belches twice more, then laughs.

"Someone looks as if they've had a good time! Depends on what? I've seen you loads of times on your own walking past my flat; how come you've never said hello?" She giggles, gently licking her lips.

"Well... considering I'm always with the Mrs... hang on, I always thought you had a fella." Tea Jay laughs and belches again.

"So, what's it going to take to get your name?" she flirts.

"Tut, I only want a bit of fun," his neighbour thinks to herself.

"It's Tea Jay! You can have a lot more than my number, if you want." His eyes move lustfully toward her tanned, stunning legs.

"So that's your Mrs, the redhead I normally see you with, pushing a pram?" she asks.

"It might be! Anyway, I've told you, my name; what's yours?" Tea Jay belches again.

"It's Debbie. Here's my number. Call me when you've sobered up," she laughs as she walks down her path.

Debbie, in her early twenties, is the kind of woman who naturally catches attention. Petite, with a light tan that highlights her toned figure, she moves with effortless grace. Her neck-length hair falls in loose waves, framing a face that's both youthful and striking. Debbie is always the centre of casual conversations with neighbours', effortlessly engaging with those around her. She radiates confidence, but there's a softness to her gaze—a subtle curiosity as she watches CJ approach. The playful flirtation in her eyes isn't lost on him, and her easy-going charm only adds to the allure. Though CJ stumbles and slurs his words, Debbie seems unbothered, amused even, as she leans against the garden fence, her laughter light and carefree.

"Absolutely and utterly Wankered!" Debbie laughs.

"Ahh, I don't know about that; my Mrs would absolutely freak. Where's your old man, anyway?" Tea Jay enquires.

"What old man's that?" Debbie asks with a smile.

Debbie's in her early twenties, quite petite with a lightly tanned figure. She has long, neck-length dark hair and lives just a few doors away from Tea Jay in the same terrace. He usually sees her chatting to her neighbours' over the fence in her front garden.

Like Tea Jay, she also lives in a one-up, one-down flat, but her flat's upstairs. She has neat ivy growing from the ground up and all around her building.

Tea Jay's practically skipping down the road, his head on cloud nine as he walks toward his path. He locks Debbie's number into his memory, then rips it up.

As he steps inside the flat, he notices that Frida's been crying, her face set like stone.

There's a suitcase packed by the front door, two red letters, and a phone bill open on the living room table.

"Eight hundred pissing quid, Tea Jay! I'm taking our son and I'm leaving you. 08 bloody 98 numbers, I see you've been up to your old tricks again, haven't you? And you've been bloody drinking; you stink of it. Just look at you—you'll never change! And don't think for a minute I didn't see you talking to that slag up the road. Well, she's pissing welcome to you," she screams, picking up their son and the suitcase before storming out.

"What did I ever see in that waster? It's just me and you now, Joseph," Frida says to herself as she walks up the road.

But if Tea Jay is honest with himself, he's secretly in his element.

"She'll be alright; a few days with her mom will do us both the world of good. Besides, I can drink openly now," a very drunk Tea Jay says to himself.

Tea Jay decides to call Debbie's number, but he suddenly becomes disheartened, thinking she gave him a bogus number because the line's dead. Then he realizes his phone's been cut off and disconnected—Frida had it disconnected.

As Tea Jay takes a drink, the drink takes him.

Tea Jay is immediately back to square one, worse than where he was in his head when he was arrested just before going to prison over a year ago.

He doesn't realize the magnitude of all the damage he's caused to himself and others. He's stuck, constantly living in the problem. Until he grasps and accepts the problem, he won't be able to live in and accept the solution.

He's trapped in a cast-iron bubble of resentment, self-pity, and blame, repeating over and over.

"If you had a life like mine, you'd fuckin' drink too."

He always finds reasons to feel sorry for himself, always looking for an excuse to drink more and more. Tea Jay is like an actor who wants to control the entire show—constantly arranging the lights, the scenery, and the other players to fit his own desires. If only everyone else would fall in line, if only things would go the way he planned, then everything would be perfect. Everyone, including himself, would be pleased. Life would be wonderful.

Sometimes, when he tries to make these arrangements, he can be quite virtuous—kind, considerate, patient, generous—even modest and self-sacrificing. On the other hand, he can be mean, egotistical, selfish, and dishonest. But like most humans, he possesses a variety of traits.

But what usually happens? The show doesn't go according to plan. He begins to think life doesn't treat him right. Admitting he may be at fault to some degree, he is sure that others are to blame. He becomes angry, indignant, self-pitying. Is he not really a self-seeker even when trying to be kind? Is he not the victim of the delusion that he can wrest satisfaction and happiness out of this world if only he manages well?

Our actor is self-centred, egocentric, as people like to call it nowadays. He is like the outlaw safe-cracker who thinks society has wronged him; and the alcoholic who has lost all and is locked up.

Selfishness, self-centeredness—that's the root of his troubles. Driven by a hundred forms of fear, self-delusion, and self-pity, Tea Jay steps on the toes of his friends and family, and they strike back.

He's desperate for love and acceptance but goes about it in all the wrong ways. He's lost in his own selfish spiral, unable to fight his way out.

Over and over, Tea Jay relives the horror from the hospital, hearing the screams when he was burned, how his right hand was destroyed by the severity of the third-degree burns.

He replays the abandonment, shuffled from one children's home to another.

Tea Jay stands still in his mind, waiting for life to hand him a miracle on a silver platter, as if standing still will solve everything.

The memories of those who should have protected him only add fuel to his anger. He remembers the beatings, the pain, and the violation he suffered in Bristol.

It's always about him—his pain, his misery.

On the verge of collapse, Tea Jay decides he's done. He swallows thirty or forty paracetamols, mixing them with booze.

As the pills take hold and more alcohol passes his lips, his stomach twists. His face contorts as he sobs uncontrollably.

"I fuckin hate you, I fuckin-bastard hate you!" he shouts, glaring at himself in the mirror.

Blinded by his pain and consumed by tunnel vision, Tea Jay refuses to see the destruction he's caused. He doesn't realize that the mirror reflects both his worst enemy and the chance for redemption.

But then, from deep inside, a quiet voice asks:

"What's your part in all of this?"

DROP THE ROCK

I t's now two weeks after Tea Jay was rushed to the hospital for a massive overdose. His family is devastated by the terrible news that he's gone.

Liz, Tea Jay's mother, is in Frida's arms at her bungalow, sobbing uncontrollably. She somewhat blames herself for what's happened to her son. She feels lost, afraid, and just wants her little boy, as he'll always be to her, to be okay. However, her desire for her son to be okay is far from the truth she'll soon realize.

Frida is a kind and loving woman, with a heart rooted in her Christian faith. She's warm and open, the type of person who would go out of her way to help others, even if it meant sacrificing her own needs.

Frida often found herself trying to fit in, sometimes becoming a target for those who took advantage of her kindness. Despite that, she carried a quiet strength and a gentle spirit that made her easy to love. Tea Jay met her through letters while in prison, and their connection initially blossomed quickly, leading to the birth of their son, Joseph. Frida brought light into TJ's life, but she was also vulnerable in ways that others could exploit.

"My poor little boy!" Tea Jay's mother sobs in front of Frida.

"Nobody forced him to do what he did. I miss him too. I can't believe he's gone and done it," Frida cries, her own tears flowing.

"I know he was a pain, but he'll always be my little boy, Frida," Liz whispers, struggling to hold back more tears.

"My little boy's gone and done himself in... we've lost him," Liz thinks, her sorrow deepening.

"I really thought he was trying to stay sober. But after that massive phone bill and him coming home drunk again, I just couldn't take it anymore," Frida explains through her tears.

"I've dealt with his antics too. But I just can't get my head around the fact that my little boy is gone," Liz breaks down again.

"I don't know how I'm going to cope with a little boy on my own," Frida cries, clinging to Liz for support.

"I still can't believe he took the easy way out. That's the coward's way!" Liz suddenly yells in frustration.

"You don't mean that, Liz... please don't say that, you don't mean it," Frida gasps, wide-eyed.

"I do mean it. He knew the pain he'd cause us all before doing this. Especially with what his own father did—leaving his boy without a father, it's beyond me. I just can't get over it," Liz screams, her frustration mixing with her grief.

Tea Jay's brother and his girlfriend, having already heard the news from Uncle Rob, enter through the front door. Even though Frida is crying in Liz's arms, Jay becomes confused and hysterical, directing his anger at Frida, blaming her for what's happened.

"Tea Jay wouldn't have taken the overdose in the first place if she hadn't left him! So why the fuck is she crying? She doesn't care he's gone. It's all her fucking fault!" Jay screams, his emotions overwhelming him.

Jay, now in his late twenties, lives with his girlfriend in central Birmingham. He's around six feet tall, with a slim build, very short ash-blonde hair, and pale skin. He has a borstal spot tattooed on his left cheek and a group of five spots on his hand. He's fashionably dressed in the latest jeans and trainers.

"Babe, calm down. She's going through enough as it is," Jay's girlfriend says softly, trying to defuse the situation.

As the house becomes increasingly chaotic with grief, Jay answers his mother's phone in the living room.

"Mom, it's a reverse charge call. The operator wants to know if we'll accept the charges!" Jay shouts toward the kitchen, where Liz is still comforting Frida.

"Tell them to piss off! If that's Lacey, I'll bloody kill her! Ask who it is, Jay," Liz yells back.

"It's Tea Jay... in Dorset," Jay responds, laughing in disbelief.

"I'll kill the little piss-ant! Give me the phone now!" Liz screams.

"Where the hell have you been? I had you dead and buried, you little shit! When the hospital told us you'd discharged yourself, we thought you'd done yourself in for good! What the hell are you doing in Poole?" Liz shouts, her anger masking her relief.

"I'm staying with a friend, Mom," Tea Jay says quietly.

"Who the hell do you know in Poole?" Liz snaps, laughing despite herself.

"We met on the chatline a while back," Tea Jay mutters, embarrassed.

"And what about Frida? You've got a son here," his mother says firmly.

"I know I have! But before you judge me, ask her about what she got up to with Jay, my own brother, when I was working nights," Tea Jay shouts, his resentment spilling out.

"Oh, that! What do you expect with the way you treated her, Tea Jay? Besides, Jay already told me. She still loves you, you know," Liz says, softening her tone.

"Why can't I just find a decent girl who won't shit on me, get a proper job, save a bit of money, and have a decent flat? Is that too much to ask, Mom?" Tea Jay whines, his voice full of self-pity.

"You and ninety-five percent of the country want the same thing, Tea Jay. But the difference is, they're willing to work for it. You expect everything handed to you on a silver platter. You need to drop that rock of blame and resentment, Tea Jay, and get yourself to AA. You need to live a sober life," Liz says, her voice a mix of love and frustration.

"It's not just your drinking, Tea; it's about identifying your part in situations, learning to stop blaming others, and altering your attitude," Tea Jay's mom thinks to herself.

"Why do I feel so lonely though, mom? I've got this void inside me, like something's missing. I've never been able to bond in any relationship because something's broken deep inside. Maybe it started when I was abused by my uncle when I was just a toddler—too young to understand. Maybe it's because of all the other stuff that happened growing up.

I get attached too quickly in relationships because of these abandonment issues, and I end up scaring women off too soon. What do you think, mom?" he snaps.

"Until you learn to love yourself, Tea Jay, and take responsibility for your actions, you'll never change. Stop living in the problem and start living in the solution. The only way you'll ever have a decent life is when you start asking for help. Go to Alcoholics Anonymous; AA worked for me," his mother pleads.

"There's too much that's happened in my life, mom, things I find hard to talk about. Stuff I've never told you, things that happened in Bristol. I blame myself for it, and I'm deeply ashamed. I get panic attacks, flashbacks, and nightmares from stuff that happened when I was a kid. Drinking helps me cope, even if it's only temporary. It drowns out the ghosts in my head, mom.

But I'm not an alcoholic. I'm just a binge drinker. I can go without it for weeks or even months," Tea Jay insists.

"But Tea Jay, when you do drink, it takes over, and you can't stop. And when you do stop, it usually ends with you in A&E or a police cell. You drink alcoholically, Tea Jay. You don't need to be a park-bench bum with a brown paper bag to be an alcoholic. Some alcoholics can go without drinking for a while, but when they do drink, they can't stop," his mother explains.

"Stop labelling me with your illness. I'm not an alcoholic," Tea Jay says, raising his voice.

"Okay, if you're not an alcoholic, then why do you never have money after drinking? Why are you in debt up to your eyeballs? You've maxed out your credit cards on booze. Why were you banned from the one-parent group? Why can't you hold down a job or a relationship? Go on, explain that. It's your life, Tea Jay.

One thing you need to do is stop blaming others and learn to drop the rock of resentment," his mother pleads.

"Look, mom, there's a good chance next week I'll be coming into thousands, absolute thousands of pounds. Then I'll ask for help, let you take me to AA, and come home," Tea Jay insists.

"Oh yeah, what've you done—robbed a bank?" she laughs.

"Well, what if I did? Don't knock it," Tea Jay says, dead serious.

A SUSPICIOUS MURDER

Tea Jay's been off his anti-psychotic medication for months now, and the voices have returned. Recently, an acquaintance informed him that the police have been asking about his whereabouts in connection with a failed post office robbery. With his personal life falling apart, his latest girlfriend threw him out after discovering his drinking habits. Now, he's back to living in a rented room, but he's behind on rent by £700 and has a week to come up with the cash or face homelessness.

Tea Jay's always been a loner, keeping to himself out of fear and mistrust. But the isolation is starting to eat at him, and he craves human connection. That's when he forms a shaky friendship with a man named Paddy, a rough-edged Irishman.

The two are constantly in and out of each other's rooms, borrowing things and sharing drinks. But after a couple of months, Tea Jay begins to see through Paddy's façade. Something about him feels off. Despite his suspicions, Tea Jay tries to brush it off, thinking he's just being paranoid.

"Hey Paddy, I'm in deep trouble. I need cash, fast. Any ideas for some quick earners?" Tea Jay asks, desperate.

Paddy's face lights up with excitement. "You into a bit of fraud, mate? I know where we can get our hands on some credit cards."

Tea Jay hesitates. There's something about using someone else's identity that gives him a fleeting sense of normality, a way to escape the trauma of his past. His identity was stripped from him long ago, during the abuse he endured as a child and later during a brutal attack in Bristol. Now, taking someone else's identity feels like a form of control, a way to feel like somebody else—anybody but himself.

"Now you're talking," Tea Jay says, his excitement growing. "So, what's the plan?"

Paddy reveals a few stolen credit cards and suggests they break into a flat upstairs, where the owner is often passed out drunk and leaves his door unlocked.

"Normally, I'd say no, but I'm desperate," Tea Jay admits, scratching his head.

"You're the right man for the job!" Paddy says with a laugh, already anticipating the reward.

Despite agreeing to the plan, Tea Jay remains suspicious of Paddy. He suspects Paddy's trying to set him up with cards that are already flagged or useless.

Paddy is a small man, barely five feet tall, with scruffy dark brown hair and a constant smell of tobacco and cheap cider. His clothes reek of sweat, and his eyes are always darting around, looking for something to take. He rents a room in the same shared house as Tea Jay, but unlike Tea Jay, Paddy's living space is a mess, littered with old food containers and dirty laundry.

Tea Jay, though struggling, keeps his room in decent shape. It's small, with a single bed, basic furniture, and worn brown curtains. But his financial situation is dire. If he doesn't find £700 soon, he'll be out on the streets just as winter sets in.

Tea Jay's room is basic but tidy, with a small bed covered in cream-colored bedding and a single wardrobe. The brown curtains look tired, and the commercial-grade brown carpet has seen better days. Still, he keeps it in order, unlike Paddy. But unless Tea Jay can come up with the rent within a few days, he'll be forced out onto the freezing cold streets of Bournemouth.

"There are some more cards on the table as you walk into the guy's flat. Let's go and have a mooch and see what we can get," Paddy says, looking visibly nervous.

"I'll take the cards, but I'll give you £100 when I've worked them," Tea Jay replies.

"Bollocks! Money now, or you get nothing, man," Paddy snaps, laughing at Tea Jay.

"Forget it, then! You'll get your cut when I've earned from them, mate," Tea Jay insists.

"So, how exactly are you going to earn from them?" Paddy asks, growing suspicious.

"That's my business, Pad. It doesn't matter how I earn, as long as I earn," Tea Jay snaps back.

Tea Jay plans to steal the guy's identity by applying for numerous store cards under the guy's name without telling Paddy.

"Take them, but don't even think about trying to have me over, Brummy," Paddy warns.

"Yeah, yeah, whatever. How many cards have you already got, then?" Tea Jay asks.

"Two," Paddy grumbles.

The next day, as Paddy is growing paranoid and furious, convinced that Tea Jay's done a runner with the cards, the old bill swarms the hostel and immediately searches Tea Jay's room.

"Fuck, that idiot got nicked, man," Paddy thinks, panicking.

Meanwhile, at the police station, as Tea Jay waits for his solicitor, two plain-clothed officers open the door to his cell, asking him again where he obtained the credit cards found in his possession.

"I'm not saying anything until I speak to my brief. Get lost!" Tea Jay snaps.

"We've given you two chances to explain where the cards came from, and all you've done is piss us around. You're not getting bail anyway, because you're already wanted. So you might as well tell us what we need to know. Attempting to obtain by deception is the least of your problems, Mr. Jay.

I'm now arresting you for murder. You do not have to say anything, but it may harm your defence if you do not mention something when questioned, which you later rely on in court. Anything you do say may be given in evidence," the officer says as he formally cautions Tea Jay once more.

"Try getting out of that one, you little prick. We've got an ace up our sleeve," the copper thinks to himself.

"What the fuck? Murder? You've got to be joking!" Tea Jay shouts, completely stunned.

Within an hour of constantly replying "no comment" in the interview, the police produce two credit cards in the victim's name, as well as a knife riddled with Tea Jay's fingerprints.

Hours later, Tea Jay is speechless as the CPS notifies the police of what Tea Jay is going to be charged with. He's remanded in police custody until the following day to appear at Bournemouth Magistrates' Court.

The knife was found wrapped in a plastic bag in the toilet tank at the same hostel where Tea Jay lives.

In his final consultation with his solicitor, Tea Jay still can't fathom how the police found his fingerprints all over a knife hidden inside the toilet tank.

BANGING UP WITH ROCKY BROWN

Tea Jay's been out of his mind on heroin and crack for the past couple of months, sinking deeper into a debt he knows he can't repay—especially to the dangerous people he's crossed. His once-functioning existence is crumbling fast.

Frida, his ex, is deeply concerned. Normally, Tea Jay would be on the phone begging for money, but this time something feels different—off.

"Have you heard from Tea Jay, Lace? I'm worried about him. He 's... he's not right," Frida asks with concern etched across her face.

"How are things with you and Jay, anyway? What's got you asking about Tea Jay?" Lacey responds, curious but guarded.

Frida tenses at the question, feeling defensive and judged about her relationship with Tea Jay's brother.

"Me and Jay are fine, Lacey. Look, when it comes to Tea Jay, he was never supportive—emotionally or financially. It was always about him—his drinking, his self-pity. He was never really there for me or our son. He's the one who ran off to Dorset, remember?"

Her mind races with insecurities. They probably think I'm a slag, leaving one brother for another...

Sensing the tension, Lacey softens her tone. "I wasn't judging, Frida. I know how hard it was for you with Tea Jay. If you're happy with my brother, that's all that matters. And no, I haven't heard from Tea Jay."

Poor Frida. She gave him chance after chance... Lacey thinks to herself.

Meanwhile, Tea Jay's physical state has deteriorated drastically. He's lost over three stone in a few months, barely eating as his addiction consumes him. With the looming possibility of a life sentence for a crime he didn't commit, the heroin and crack become his only solace, dulling the weight of his ever-darkening future.

One morning, after smoking crack, panic grips him. He's struggling to breathe, gasping as his chest tightens. He tries to shout for help, but his voice barely escapes as he hyperventilates. His breath is shallow, laboured.

Through the cast-iron door of his cell, he hears the familiar voice of a prison officer, one he has a history with.

"You idiot! What did you expect, smoking that stuff? You're talking, so you're breathing. Look at the state of you. You're a fool to yourself," the officer shouts through the door.

Tea Jay can barely respond, but he spits out, "Oh yeah, what do you know, gov? You're fine, aren't ya? You've got your nice house, wife, kids. I've got a habit, boss... a fuckin' habit!"

The officer, unbothered by Tea Jay's outburst, sighs. "You only give me lip because I tell you the truth, and you can't face it. You need help.

This is the same as a couple of months ago, Tea Jay. Don't you see the pattern?"

The officer's voice softens. "I've been there too, mate. I did the booze and cocaine. Maybe I don't have a criminal record like you, but I could have if I hadn't asked for help."

The officer stands just outside Tea Jay's cell, his expression one of frustration but concern. He's around the same height as Tea Jay, five foot nine, with a muscular frame and the distinct smell of Kouros cologne.

"If you don't seek help, this is going to be your life, over and over, until it kills you. Is that what you want?"

Tea Jay, exhausted and shaking from the drugs, manages to look up. "Gov, I had you all wrong. I thought you were a wanker, but you're not that bad, are ya? I do need help. But what kind of help can I get in here?"

The officer nods, his eyes showing a flicker of empathy. "I'll talk to the CARAT team and see what we can do."

"Cheers, gov," Tea Jay whispers, his body shivering as withdrawal kicks in.

Suddenly, a wave of dread washes over him, freezing him in place. His mind flashes back to a terrifying acid trip he had once, and an eerie voice echoes in his head: What's your part in all this?

Did I just say that? Tea Jay questions himself, shaken.

Left alone in his cell, the sickness grips him harder, and he begins vomiting uncontrollably through the night. He knows the next seven days will be hell. He's already dreading the weekend ahead, knowing he'll barely be able to eat or drink. In desperation, he bangs on the door, asking for milk—the only thing he can keep down.

Tea Jay shivers uncontrollably, alternating between hot and cold sweats throughout the weekend. His nights are soaked in sweat, leaving his sheets drenched and sticky. By morning, he wakes up to an even worse situation—diarrhoea covering both him and his bed.

Locked away from society in the harsh reality of the block, Tea Jay knows that one wrong move could land him in even deeper trouble. Trapped within the confines of not just the prison, but the prison of his own mind, he constantly struggles to separate reality from his drug-fuelled hallucinations.

Life in the block is brutal. There are no personal possessions to provide comfort, just a filthy prison kit and a coarse towel. The bed is nothing more than a concrete slab with a thin mattress, and every piece of furniture is bolted to the floor or walls to prevent prisoners from using them as weapons or barricades.

"Gov, why can't I open the fuckin' window in here? It stinks, boss. I've been sick all night long. C'mon, I need some fresh air," Tea Jay groans, clutching his stomach. "And don't get the block orderly to touch my bedding. I've got diarrhoea all over it."

"If it were up to me, I'd make you sleep in that filth, you dirty rat," snaps an officer, glancing at the disgruntled orderly assigned to clean the cell.

"Dirty smackhead," the orderly mutters under his breath, reluctantly stepping into the stench-filled cell.

"I can't help it, gov," Tea Jay pleads, his voice cracking.

"Can't help it, my arse. You lot are all the same. Get in the shower—you're up for adjudication this morning," the officer barks, glaring at the dishevelled prisoner. "I suppose someone forced that shit into you, huh?"

As Tea Jay writhes in his cell, withdrawal biting into his bones, the realization hits harder than any physical pain—Paddy and Karen had played him. The intrusive thoughts circle like vultures: Karen, once his girl, now wrapped around Paddy's finger, and Paddy, always whis-

pering lies, setting him up for a fall. That knife, hidden in the toilet urn—the very knife Paddy had given him—had his fingerprints all over it. And Karen, sweet, treacherous Karen, was in on it from the start, selling him out without a second thought.

The credit cards, the lies, it all starts to make sickening sense. They wanted him out of the picture. The betrayal burns more than the rattling in his veins. Tea Jay's stomach turns, not just from the detox but from the cruel twist of fate. Trapped behind bars, with Karen and Paddy free, walking the streets, laughing at how easily they'd set him up. They had taken everything.

"C'mon, gov, I'm serious—I want to get clean," Tea Jay says, trying to sound sincere.

"If I had a pound for every time I heard that, I'd be retired by now," the officer scoffs, shaking his head.

Later that morning, Tea Jay finds himself standing before the prison governor. Two young, muscular officers flank him, their eyes burning with intensity, ready to pounce at the slightest sign of resistance.

After pleading guilty to assaulting an officer, Tea Jay receives twenty-eight days loss of remission and a further fourteen days in the block, with a month's loss of all privileges. He stands there, trying to process the weight of it all.

His stomach churns with worry. He knows he owes money to the other prisoners on his landing, and the only way he was able to pay them back was by smuggling drugs in from visits. But now, with all his privileges revoked for at least two weeks, he's in deeper trouble than ever. Back on the wing, the debtors will be waiting for him.

Tea Jay considers the one option he dreads most—requesting to go on the numbers for protection. However, when he finally makes the request, it's denied. The prison is overcrowded, packed to the rafters, with only three wings: one for convicted prisoners, one for those on remand, and the third for those on Rule 43—prisoners needing protection, known as "the numbers."

The numbers are where the vulnerable go. It's where informants, debtors, and those convicted of heinous crimes seek refuge from the general population. Tea Jay knows the stigma, but with mounting threats, he's left with no choice.

Three weeks later, after serving his time in the block, Tea Jay returns to the wing. One morning, he finds a chit slipped under his door—he's got a special visit next week. A chill runs down his spine. He knows it can only mean one thing: the police.

Rattled and anxious, he seeks out another con who's just come back from a visit with a parcel.

"Mate, can you tick me a bag till next week?" Tea Jay asks, desperation in his voice.

"Fuck you, you mug; you're getting nothing from me, mate," the other con snarls as he head-butts Tea Jay in the nose.

"Yow, what was that for?" Tea Jay growls.

The con is extremely angry, almost growling; he's about five feet ten, very muscular, with a bald head and a tattoo of a swastika on his neck. He's pale-skinned, with borstal spots on each knuckle and several other tattoos, including a star on the other side of his neck.

"What, you think just because those geezers who you owed money to have walked out, you've escaped the debt? You're dreaming, mate! You think you can have us over too? That debt is ours now, you little rat. You're lucky to be alive and not hot-watered or striped, you prick. You owe us £200, and we want it within two weeks. Count yourself lucky," the con snarls.

Two weeks later, Tea Jay's in serious trouble, again up the creek without a paddle. He tries to outsmart his creditors by applying to go on the numbers, but they've found out, leaving him to wonder if they've bribed a screw. Even if he's dodged them before, he knows there's nowhere to run in jail.

After managing to plug half an ounce of gear on a visit, he breathes a sigh of relief as he waits in his cell for the blokes he owes, both of whom are at work. However, when he attempts to leave his cell, he's overpowered by a couple of cons rushing in with sheets over their heads.

Tea Jay is hit hard in the jaw, leaving him dazed.

They hold him down, and he feels a large object pushed into him to retrieve the drugs he had plugged earlier; then his attackers quickly leave. In the scuffle, he recognizes a tattoo on one of them—only a cleaner could have done this. Despite the pain, he knows he can't report it; he believes he's being set up and decides he must take drastic action.

Prison isn't a fairytale, and he knows he's as good as dead anyway.

"Fucking hell, I'm a dead man. I've got second-degree murder looming over me, and I'll be straight back on remand once this sentence is over; fuck it," Tea Jay thinks, head in his hands.

The next day in the exercise yard, Tea Jay approaches both cleaners who attacked him in his cell.

In plain view of the screws, he casually walks up to them and fires two quick punches, knocking both of them out cold. Neither the screws nor the orderlies saw it coming.

Suddenly, screws come from everywhere as the riot bell blares.

The following day, Tea Jay walks around his cell in the block when one of the screws comes to collect him for a special visit with the police.

He thinks they're there to question him about the attack on the exercise yard.

However, they ask him vague questions about someone from the same hostel in Bournemouth and about the Irish guy who lived there. Tea Jay keeps quiet. The police then inform him they're not pursuing the murder case and have charged someone else.

"Fuck-in-hell! I've just knocked out a couple of geezers, thinking I had nothing to lose. Oh, for fuck's sake. What the fuck have I done?" Tea Jay screams, throwing his blue plastic mug at the wall.

An hour later, after being taken back to the block.

"You're facing outside court for this, you know that, don't you? You've broken one of the cleaners' jaws in three places," the prison officer says.

"Three places? I only hit the guy once, boss," Tea Jay sighs.

Two days later, he's charged with GBH under Section 18 – Wounding with intent against one of the cleaners.

Tea Jay appears in magistrates court via video link a few days later, where he's informed, he'll automatically be remanded in custody once his original prison sentence ends in two weeks.

However, he argues that since he only hit the guy once, it should be reduced to GBH under Section 20.

A month later, he's managed to get on the numbers due to fears for his life. As he lays on his bunk, one of the prison probation officers comes to interview him about the possibility of a drug treatment and testing order (DTTO).

"I'm not going to get a DTTO because I'm on remand for assault. You only get one of those if you're in for drugs, boss," Tea Jay argues.

"Let me worry about that, shall we?" the probation officer replies.

A GOLDEN
OPPURTUNITY

T wo drug and alcohol counsellors visit Tea Jay to interview him, assessing his suitability for a DTTO (Drug Treatment and Testing Order). Both are friendly and welcoming, creating an unexpectedly calming presence.

The first is a woman, around five feet nine, the same height as Tea Jay. She has grey-blonde hair tied in a ponytail, her pale complexion suggesting she's seen her share of hard days. She's slim, almost gaunt, dressed in a white floral summer dress with white trainers. A faint hint of patchouli oil lingers around her, giving her a hippyish vibe.

The second counsellor is a thickset man, likely in his late forties. His hair is receding, almost bald, and he wears a green Adidas pullover, blue Levi's, and similar white trainers. Both of them sound like they're from the South East of England.

"So, what's the main issue, Tea Jay?" the female counsellor asks.

Tea Jay half-believes this could be his ticket to avoid more prison time, but something deeper within him is crying out for help. He's mentally and spiritually shattered, every part of him broken.

With a deep look of melancholy, he begins recounting his upbringing.

The counsellor gently cuts him off, saying, "There'll be plenty of time to talk about your past if you get the DTTO. Right now, let's focus on the present."

"Sorry, I just thought I'd break the ice," Tea Jay says, deflecting. "What do you actually want to know?"

"What's the main problem, Tea Jay?" she asks patiently.

He pauses, then starts again, his voice low and broken.

"It started with the booze, but it didn't stop there. I ended up banging up with the rock and brown. When I thought I was facing life for that post office murder, I started chasing the dragon to block out the thought of a life sentence. Got into a lot of debt with the stone, and then some of the cons I owed injected me with brown to keep me hooked... to keep me in debt."

The counsellor listens quietly, her eyes revealing understanding but not sympathy. She knows the issue runs deeper than the substances. She leans in slightly.

"If we accept you into treatment, you have to be willing to go to any lengths. Are you willing, Tea Jay?"

"Yeah, of course. One hundred percent," he replies, almost too quickly.

"The treatment can be intense. What do you think we can do for you?" she asks.

"Help me stay clean and sober," Tea Jay says, but even he knows it's not the full truth.

"Is that what you really want? To stay clean?"

"Nah, I want a nice girlfriend, a job, and some money saved up," Tea Jay blurts out.

"That's all external stuff, Tea Jay. What do you really want?" she presses gently.

"For fuck's sake, they're speaking in riddles," Tea Jay thinks, frustrated. "I just want to stay off the booze and brown."

Finally, he says aloud, "I need help." His voice cracks, and tears well up in his eyes.

The counsellor softens. "Tell me about the attack in the yard," she asks, her voice calm but firm. "Just give me the basic details."

Tea Jay clenches his jaw. "Those idiots deserved what they got," he thinks but responds differently.

"I owed more than £200 in drug debts, and they were making me smuggle gear into the nick. After a visit, I got robbed, viciously attacked. I thought I was being set up, so I lashed out. I thought I had nothing left to lose."

Tears run down his face now, unbidden.

Tea Jay's section 18 charge for grievous bodily harm with intent was dropped to GBH section 20—a much lesser charge. At sentencing, the judge addresses him directly.

"I'm sentencing you to a six-month drug treatment and testing order, alongside a twelve-month probation order, Mr. Jay. You have a golden opportunity here. Breach it, and I won't be so lenient next time. You'll report monthly for review. Good luck."

With his bus fare in hand, Tea Jay heads for the bail hostel. He should feel grateful for avoiding a heavy sentence, but something gnaws at him.

"Something's looking out for me," he thinks. "Me hitting those cleaners—it was meant to be. I asked for help, and now I'm getting it."

But as the thought settles in, like a thunderbolt, a darker one follows: You would've died alone if they'd released you after that last sentence.

"Where the fuck did that come from?" Tea Jay shivers.

Entering the bail hostel in Dorset, he's greeted by a familiar face. Someone he'd done time with before walks straight up, arms open.

"Hello, mate! Give us a hug!"

Tea Jay stiffens, taken aback. He barely knows the guy.

"What the fuck?" Tea Jay mutters under his breath.

The guy's name is Stu. He's local, like most of the people in the hostel, and also on a DTTO. Stu's about five foot five, with a cleft lip and short, dark brown hair. He dresses stylishly, always in the latest casual clothes and trainers. What strikes Tea Jay most, though, is that there's something different about Stu's eyes—he seems unusually happy.

The next day, Tea Jay and some of his new friends make it to the treatment center with minutes to spare. Another client is already in the office for a drug test. Tea Jay, still under the illusion that this might be a place of pampering and relaxation, is in for a shock.

He's introduced to his key worker, John, one of the counsellors who visited him six weeks earlier.

"You need to provide a urine sample for testing," John says flatly, "and we'll also need to strip search you before we proceed. It's standard procedure."

Tea Jay isn't surprised. He figures plenty of people must try smuggling contraband into the centre, so he complies without issue.

"We also take a Polaroid for a before-and-after photo," John continues, "so clients can see the difference from when they enter treatment to graduation."

The treatment centre itself is nothing like Tea Jay imagined. It's on a corner of a main road, its entrance controlled by a locked door and intercom. Once inside, the place is stark. To the right is a kitchen with a microwave and tea-making facilities for break times. Directly ahead are two small interview rooms and toilets, while a door to the left leads to the main group room, where thirty chairs are arranged in a circle. This is where group sessions, like the Monday morning "grassing group," are held.

After his photo is taken, Tea Jay is handed an intrusive-looking questionnaire. He's told to complete it, along with a life story, within a few days. He mentions his struggles with punctuation, but John dismisses it. "Ask the other clients for help. It's your responsibility to get it done."

Tea Jay's frustration bubbles up. "Fuckin' prick," he thinks.

In his first group session, things go downhill quickly. One of the girls is sharing about her past and addiction, but Tea Jay interrupts, talking over her and slipping into blame mode. Another client from the local area challenges him, accusing him of putting on an act.

"What, you think you know me?" Tea Jay snaps. "You don't know shit. I remember you; you and your mate screwed me over."

"Quieten down," says Eddie, one of the counsellors. "You two obviously have unresolved issues, but this isn't the time. We'll deal with it after the session."

"I'll smash your head in the carpark unless you apologize," the other client, Richard, says, stepping forward aggressively.

"I'm not apologizing for shit. You and your mate ripped me off," Tea Jay snarls.

Eddie steps in again, keeping things calm. "Tea Jay, you need to apologize to Rachel for interrupting her share."

Tea Jay grumbles, "Sorry, Rachel."

Richard storms out of the session, shouting that he's never coming back. Deep down, Tea Jay feels a twisted satisfaction—he's glad to see the back of Richard, even if he's far from acknowledging his own part in their falling out.

The day proves to be heavy. In the "Concerns" group, two people are discharged and breached for using drugs. After being pointed out by other clients, they initially deny it, but breath and drug tests tell a different story. They're immediately asked to leave.

The last session of the day is the "feelings" meeting, where each person shares how they're feeling. Before they can leave for the day, one of the counsellors asks what AA or NA meeting each client plans to attend that evening, reminding them that attendance is mandatory. They're also required to buddy up with another client until graduation.

After a few days at the bail hostel, Tea Jay begins his Therapeutic Daily Duties (TDs). He knows compliance is the key to staying out of prison, so he goes through the motions, but he doesn't yet grasp the deeper meaning of the program. He doesn't realize that this is more than just staying clean—it's about complete surrender, letting go of blame, resentment, and the victim mentality.

Tea Jay must drop the rock of blame if he's ever going to be "rocketed" into the fourth dimension of hope. The sooner he embraces an attitude of gratitude, the better his chances of survival.

One of the other clients, acting suspiciously, approaches Tea Jay, reeking of raw garlic. The stench of alcohol is unmistakable.

"I bet you think I'm just some pushover? Well, grass me up and I'll fuckin snap your neck. You get me?" the man hisses, his eyes full of threat.

Tea Jay isn't the only one having trouble with this particular bully. Earlier that morning, one of his peers had a similar encounter.

"Enough of this," Stu thinks to himself. "I'm not going to let some prick of a bully wreck my chances of staying clean and risk getting breached for keeping quiet. That puts everyone at risk."

Tea Jay and Stu agree to inform the treatment centre staff, knowing that silence is enabling the bully, which itself is a breach able offense.

Meanwhile, Richard, the peer who clashed with Tea Jay the previous day, returns to the centre to apologize. They step outside with one of the counsellors for a cigarette and a conversation.

"Are you alright, Tea Jay?" Richard asks.

"I'm sorry, Rich. I didn't understand the rules about sharing yesterday when I interrupted that girl. I thought you were trying to show me up. That's why I snapped," Tea Jay says, trying to justify his reaction.

Richard doesn't buy it. "You're a long way from making genuine amends if you're just going to make excuses for yourself," he snaps back, just as the counsellor intervenes.

"Tea Jay, making amends isn't about justifying your behaviour. It's about owning your part in it. The other person's actions don't matter—you need to take responsibility and apologize for what you did, and move forward," John says gently.

"What have I done now?" Tea Jay thinks, confused and frustrated.

Afterward, Tea Jay is called for another urine test before the day's first group session, where one peer shares their story, and others offer feedback or reflect on their own recoveries. When it's Tea Jay's turn, he tries to pass. But a counsellor insists that sharing is crucial not only for his recovery but for helping others as well.

"This place is hardcore," Tea Jay mutters during the break.

"You've seen nothing yet," one of the peers laughs.

The next session is a Reiki group for relaxation. The facilitator explains chakras and places crystals on the peers while they lie down

168 E J MARSH

to relax. Tea Jay falls asleep and starts snoring, causing the others to laugh. When he wakes up startled, the facilitator reassures him that sleeping is a good sign—it shows he was able to relax and let go.

Later, a sense of celebration fills the centre as one of the peers graduates from primary treatment. After completing twelve weeks, she's moving into secondary housing—a huge milestone. As everyone gathers, the peer tearfully compares her "before" and "after" photos, seeing the transformation. The room erupts in applause as she receives her certificate and graduation plaque.

Before the day ends, each client is asked to share affirmations about themselves—statements they struggle to believe but need to embrace for recovery. They're also reminded to attend mandatory meetings that evening. The counsellors often do spot checks, making sure everyone is where they should be.

At an NA meeting later that night, Tea Jay becomes distracted by a beautiful woman, lusting after her almost immediately. In his mind, he confuses lust with love and becomes fixated on the idea of being liked, loved, and accepted. He's prone to giving women anything they ask for, leaving himself open to psychological manipulation, all in the desperate hope of being wanted.

This emotional vulnerability leaves Tea Jay restless, irritable, and discontent. He's looking for the quick fix, the sense of ease and comfort, but his lack of self-esteem and understanding of healthy relationships only leads him deeper into confusion and pain.

Tea Jay's world flips upside down whenever he meets a woman, as he tends to wear his heart on his sleeve. He becomes co-dependent, demanding, and desperate for their constant attention, ultimately scaring them away, fearing they'll abandon him like everyone else.

The ache inside him grows unbearable, and he craves the sense of ease and comfort that only alcohol seems to provide. Seeing others drink without consequence reminds him why he's not ready for a relationship, despite his longing for one.

Later that evening, during an AA meeting, Tea Jay overhears a shocking piece of news. One of his peers has died from drinking high-proof white rum.

"I thought they were missing from the treatment centre today," Tea Jay gasps, stunned by the suddenness of it.

A dark thought crosses his mind: One minute you're here, and the next, the lights go out, and you're gone.

Someone else at the meeting comments, "When you join AA, you need two things: a Big Book and a black tie. You'll need them both eventually."

The following day, the treatment centre staff decide to hold a feelings meeting at the start of the day instead of the usual time.

"Why are we doing this now?" a client asks.

"Just take your seat," a counsellor instructs.

"How are you feeling, Kate?" the counsellor asks one of the clients.

"I'm upset—hearing that one of my peers is dead..." Kate says, her voice trembling as she looks down.

"What does 'upset' feel like, Kate? Can you describe it?"

"Afraid. Alone. Heartbroken," she says, finally breaking down into tears.

A counsellor then addresses the room, explaining how someone who graduated only two months ago believed it was safe to drink again after time away from alcohol. They thought they were cured but instead fell into the trap of addiction once more.

"Once an alcoholic, always an alcoholic," the counsellor reminds them.

For weeks, the news weighs heavily on everyone. Slowly, life at the centre returns to normal.

"I can't believe she's gone," one client says.

"Well, at least you're still here. Learn from it," a friend of the deceased replies. "She stopped going to meetings after she graduated. She didn't want to do Step Four and ignored her sponsor's advice. She wasn't being honest with herself and put everything ahead of her recovery. After her relationship ended, she couldn't handle the pain, took a drink, and now... she's gone."

"The pain is in the avoidance," a counsellor chimes in.

"What do you mean?" asks a client.

"If you avoid your problems, they'll never go away. You can't heal what you refuse to face. Let go, let God. Hurt people hurt people."

Almost two months later, Tea Jay stands before the judge at his third review. He's congratulated for his progress and looks visibly healthier. A week later, he receives more good news—he's set to graduate the following week and will move into a shared house right after.

Tea Jay is ecstatic at the thought of leaving the treatment centre.

"No more walking around in twos. No more boring TDs. No more intrusive groups. And I can go to meetings when I feel like it," he thinks, breathing a sigh of relief. "At least the shared house isn't staffed. Bliss!"

At his graduation, Tea Jay can't help but smile at the stark contrast between his "before" and "after" Polaroids. But as the applause dies down, a knot forms in his stomach. He's grown accustomed to being protected, wrapped in cotton wool, and safe within the treatment centre's walls.

Though he looks great on the outside, inside, he's still full of anger, resentment, and turmoil.

At an AA meeting that evening, another member shares, "You can look good on the outside, but if nothing changes on the inside, nothing changes. It's an inside job."

The speaker continues, "It's not just about going through the steps—it's about change."

As Tea Jay prepares to leave the safety of the centre, fear begins to creep in. The thought of fending for himself terrifies him. He wishes he'd listened to his counsellors' and girlfriend about getting a support worker to help with budgeting and managing his life outside.

A month later, Tea Jay's life begins to unravel. Despite having a roof over his head, he's running out of money, has no food, and his debts are piling up. He's stopped going to meetings, doesn't have a sponsor, and some of his old, dishonest ways of thinking are creeping back in.

As he contemplates unrealistic ways to make quick money, a familiar, insidious voice whispers in his mind:

"You're fixed now. You don't need AA. Go on, just have a couple of beers. No one will know."

THE WHIRLWIND

"Hey sis, I've met this lovely guy outside the shop; I think he might be just what I need," Kaz says to her sister, her voice both hopeful and anxious, betraying a mix of excitement and trepidation.

Karen studies her sister's face, sensing the familiar pattern—the rush to see every new man as an answer to her prayers. Still, for a brief moment, it's as though some of Kaz's inner turmoil is soothed.

"I don't blame you, especially after the way that dickhead you're with has been treating you. So, what's his name?" her sister asks, raising an eyebrow, concerned but curious.

"Yeah, I haven't had much luck with blokes, have I, sis?" Kaz replies, her voice edged with weariness from too many failed attempts.

Their conversation is interrupted by another call from Tea Jay. Karen's sister throws her a disapproving look, noticing how often he's been ringing her.

"He's calling again? Seriously, Kaz, that's a bit much," Karen sighs, a hint of frustration seeping into her tone.

Karen's sister knows how easily Kaz falls too hard and too fast. She can see it all unravelling already. "It's going to end in tears," she thinks, her instincts warning her that this man is trouble, just like the others.

"Tea Jay, you don't need to call me four times in one day," Karen says as she picks up the phone, trying to maintain her patience. "I said I'd meet you outside the shop later."

"I just can't stop thinking about you. I've never met anyone like you before, Kaz. You're definitely going to meet me, right?" Tea Jay's voice is filled with desperation.

"Yes, I said I would, didn't I?" Karen stresses, wondering if this is already heading down the wrong path. "Oh no, not again. I hope I haven't found another one like that last guy. Still, I'd do anything to get away from the mess I'm in now."

Kaz is an assistant manager at a clothing hire shop. Outwardly, she seems to have her life together, but deep down, she's still running from the same chaos she's always known.

Tea Jay, on the other hand, tends to scare most women off with his intensity. He falls in love too quickly, always chasing a connection that will somehow fix the emptiness inside him. His insecurities make him clingy, obsessive—traits that have driven women away before. He calls constantly, his stomach knotted with anxiety, because all he knows is the pain of abandonment and rejection.

"I hope I haven't scared her off. She's different; she's got to be the one," Tea Jay thinks, unable to calm the storm of worry swirling inside him.

"Karen, don't let men walk all over you, especially not at the beginning. Relationships should be about balance, not control. You need someone who cares for you, not someone who makes you feel trapped," her sister advises, her voice tinged with a mix of concern and frustration.

Karen knows her sister is right, but part of her is desperate for this to work. "He sounds so obsessed already," Leanne thinks, keeping her opinions mostly to herself. "Kaz always goes for the wrong guys, and this one seems no different."

Six weeks later, Karen and Tea Jay seem to be inseparable, but the cracks are starting to show.

"Sis, I can't take it anymore. I've got to get away from here. He's really starting to wear me down," Karen confesses, exhaustion evident in her voice.

"Then leave him. You've already got someone else. Move on," her sister urges, though she knows how hard it is for Karen to walk away.

"It's just... he drinks like a fish, snorts coke like there's no tomorrow, and he reeks of weed all the time," Karen complains, feeling trapped in another cycle of dysfunction.

Karen and her twin sister Leanne are identical, right down to their matching wardrobes. They share everything, including their bad luck with men. Both of them tend to fall for the wrong kind of guys, despite their best efforts

Two weeks later, Karen asks Tea Jay for help in finding a new place to live.

"Fancy helping me find a new flat? I've got to get away from him, Tea Jay," Karen pleads, her voice tinged with desperation.

"Yeah, definitely!" Tea Jay replies, thrilled to have the chance to play the saviour. "Hang on... are you asking me to move in with you?" he adds excitedly.

"I might be," Karen teases, though in truth, she's just desperate to escape her current situation. "I've got to get away from that house. I can't stand it anymore," she thinks, feeling suffocated.

Two weeks later, they find a place within the Dorset area and move in together immediately. They're constantly in each other's pockets, day in and day out, their lives so entangled that it's hard to tell where one ends and the other begins. Tea Jay even convinces Karen to open a credit card account and gives him an additional card.

Their flat is a one-bedroom place just behind a bus station, but surprisingly, the noise isn't an issue. What is an issue, however, is the string of bars surrounding their home, just within throwing distance. For Tea Jay, they're a temptation he knows he shouldn't entertain, but the allure is always there, pulling him toward old habits.

A couple of months after moving in, Tea Jay proposes to Karen, presenting her with an expensive gold ring he bought using her credit card. She's overjoyed, and they tie the knot quickly, neither of them pausing to consider the consequences of their rushed decisions.

Two weeks later, Tea Jay finds a job, but it doesn't last. He turns up to work drunk, stumbling around the site, and after a heated brawl with an enraged site manager, he's fired.

A couple of days later, Tea Jay bumps into an old acquaintance from prison. Mike, a scrappy, muscular guy with a deep northern accent, short dark hair, and piercing blue eyes, seems down on his luck. Feeling a sense of misplaced loyalty, Tea Jay invites him back to his place, where Karen surprisingly welcomes him with open arms.

"You can use some of my clothes until you get sorted, Mike. But remember, this is temporary until you find your own place," Tea Jay says firmly, trying to set boundaries.

Karen, however, seems much more inviting. "Don't be like that, Tea Jay. You're welcome to stay as long as you like, sweetheart. Don't listen to him," she laughs, clearly charmed by Mike.

Within days, Tea Jay regrets the decision. Mike borrows money, exaggerates stories of his supposed criminal empire, and spends too much time talking to Karen. Suspicion gnaws at Tea Jay, who starts feeling pushed out of his own home.

One night, after coming home drunk with Mike, Tea Jay stumbles
through the door. The smell of alcohol and sweat clings to him as
Karen glares. A heated argument erupts, accusations flying. Before
long, in a fit of rage, Tea Jay yanks off his wedding ring and throws
it at her.

He hits the clubs, drowning his anger in alcohol, and by the time he
returns home in the early hours, the front door is locked. Anger flares
up again. He pounds on the door, kicks it, yells, and punches it until
the neighbours call the police.

Tea Jay is arrested for criminal damage and drunk and disorderly
behaviour, but in his drunken stupor, he decides to lash out at one
of the officers, earning him an additional charge of assaulting police.
Pepper spray stings his eyes as he's taken down and cuffed.

As he sobers up in the cold cell, his head pounds and reality sinks
in. He's on the cold stone floor, with nothing but a thin blue plastic
mattress. His dirty shirt clings to his sweaty back, and the smell of stale
alcohol fills the small space.

Tears stream down his face. "Why did I let that prick talk me into
having a drink? Why's he lying to my wife, trying to get into her
knickers?" Tea Jay's mind spins with rage, self-pity, and regret.

He stumbles out of the police station hours later after being granted
bail, his mind clouded with a mix of anger and self-loathing. As he
walks home, he spots something glinting from a small hedge. He peers
closer—it's the shiny barrel of a gun, half-hidden under some cloth.

"That's a gun, that is. Who's in charge now?" he mutters under
his breath, as a surge of bitterness courses through him. The weight
of the world presses down on him, dragging him deeper into a pit of
self-destruction.

When TJ first met Karen, it was almost by accident—she needed
help bolting the top of her door, and he was there to assist. What start-

ed as a simple gesture quickly turned into a whirlwind romance. She became his escape, an answer to the void he carried inside, but TJ was too consumed by his own demons—his drinking, his dishonesty—to truly love her. She had a heart of gold, but even that wasn't enough to save him from himself.

Lost in his thoughts, Tea Jay's mind spirals with violent ideas, each one darker than the last. His footsteps slow, weighed down by anger and confusion. But as he rounds the corner, his gaze locks onto two familiar figures walking hand in hand in the distance. His breath catches. His steps falter.

A wave of disbelief washes over him, leaving him frozen mid-step, heart pounding, unsure of what to do next.

CRAWLING THROUGH THE MUD

J ay, Tea Jay's brother, has had to flee Birmingham in a hurry. Apart from being wanted by the police, someone has tried to kill both him and his brother.

There's no time to think. Jay grabs nothing but the clothes on his back and bolts. With no money, he jumps the train, just like Tea Jay. Meanwhile, Tea Jay uses his credit card—the one that only seems to work onboard trains—to buy a ticket to Bournemouth.

Tea Jay is in no better shape than his brother. He only has the clothes he's wearing, and his ex-wife has given away all his belongings to her new man. The guy even wears Tea Jay's old wedding ring, the one his ex-wife gladly passed on.

"Fuck 'em all," Tea Jay thinks, bitterness settling into his bones. "If she can abandon me, why the hell should I care about stealing? If she doesn't care, neither do I."

It's 2002, and the brothers reunite down south.

Some would call it luck—others would say something entirely different—but they somehow manage to get hold of a two-man tent, a groundsheet, and camping essentials that they "find" behind a camping shop in town.

Needletown is a picturesque place on the south coast, known for its golden-sandy beaches and lively nightlife. But beneath the surface, it's riddled with drugs, knife crime, and the kind of darkness that thrives in the shadows.

To the locals, Needletown is "the armpit of the universe."

As Tea Jay walks through the town, he tells Jay to meet him by the local library in a few hours. He's got a plan to get his hands on some quick cash, though he hasn't considered the consequences of his actions.

That afternoon, Tea Jay strolls into Debenhams, a packed department store, and applies for instant credit using stolen details. The application goes through, and within minutes, he's walking out with £1,250 worth of gift vouchers and a change of clothes for both himself and Jay.

After selling the vouchers for £500 to an old contact, they waste no time looking for something to take the edge off—the booze isn't cutting it anymore.

"Where can we score, bro?" Tea Jay asks.

"Easy. We'll hit up a couple of homeless guys for a dealer's number," Jay replies.

Within hours, they've got their hands on gear—heroin, pins, citric acid—and they're back in their tent.

"You okay with this?" Jay asks, eyeing the needles. "I don't want you going over."

"I've done it before in jail," Tea Jay snaps. "Just hurry up."

His eyes sparkle with anticipation, his mouth dry with the craving. He doesn't think about the risks—overdosing, suffocating, dying. None of that matters right now.

He pricks his vein with a quarter of the bag, and the familiar wave of warmth floods his body.

"Ahh, thank fuck for that," he mutters as the heroin takes hold, delivering its brutal, intoxicating peace.

But it doesn't take long for things to sour. Later that night, Tea Jay catches Jay taking more than his share. Rage explodes inside him, and he punches his brother square in the face, knocking him out cold.

By morning, they're often still out of it from the heroin, gouching-out in the tent pitched on a cliffside, oblivious to the world around them.

Three months pass. Tea Jay is barely recognizable, thin as a skeleton, reeking of the streets, yet he keeps going. He continues scamming for instant credit, walking into stores like he owns the place.

But luck eventually runs out. This time, as he walks out with stolen goods, someone follows him. He's apprehended, arrested, and taken to the station.

In the cell, they strip-search him. The marks on his arms and groin, the gaunt look in his eyes, and the unmistakable smell of heroin tell them all they need to know.

Tea Jay has hit rock bottom.

Hours later, Tea Jay begins to rattle hard, making a racket in his cell as he shouts for the doctor, begging for DF 118s to numb the pain. But no one comes. His cries echo off the cold walls, met only with silence and indifference.

Eventually, after what feels like an eternity, he's released on bail. They give him 47/3 bail, meaning he has to return to the station in six weeks for further questioning.

Meanwhile, Jay is losing his mind. He's pacing the streets, frantic with worry, fearing his brother has scored in the toilets somewhere and overdosed.

He starts to cry.

Despite everything, they're still brothers. They've always been all each other has.

"Where the hell are you, brow? You better be okay... and you better have some gear when I find you." Jay mutters to himself, fists clenched.

The next day, after being bailed out, Tea Jay stumbles through the streets. He's really panicking because his brother isn't in the tent. He's filthy, soaked in sweat, and shaking uncontrollably. His stomach is twisted in knots, and he vomits on the sidewalk, gagging from the pain of withdrawal.

Desperation hits him as he searches for a place to relieve himself. Finding no other option, he ducks behind a bush, writhing in agony, too constipated to find relief. His body is a mess, and his mind is shattered.

For a fleeting moment, shame flickers in his thoughts, but it's quickly swallowed by the haze of addiction. The heroin has taken everything from him—his pride, his dignity, his self-worth.

"I've got to get off this shit. I can't live like this anymore," Tea Jay mutters, staring into the dirt beneath him.

Two days later, Tea Jay still has no clue where Jay is. His nerves are shot, and the gnawing fear that his brother might be dead is driving him to the edge. As he walks, he overhears two homeless men talking about a guy from the Midlands who overdosed and died on the streets. Tea Jay can't help but wonder if it's just gossip, but the gnawing fear that it could be true claws at his chest.

Tears well up in Tea Jay's eyes, and just as he's about to break down, a voice calls out from behind him.

"Brow! Where the hell have you been? I got nicked, and when I got bailed, I thought you were dead! Some winos were saying a guy from Brum OD'd in the park. I was losing my mind," Tea Jay blurts out.

"I thought you'd gone over too, brow," Jay replies, relief evident in his voice. "But hey, I met a couple of working girls. They'll pay us in bags if we keep an eye out for them while they work."

Tea Jay smirks, the familiar pull of the game too tempting to resist. "Yeah, man. Let's go."

Four months pass, and Tea Jay and Jay have settled into their bleak routine, watching the girls in the park as they work, ducking the police who constantly patrol the streets, shaking down anyone they suspect. Tea Jay's addiction has escalated. He's often seen carrying a Glock, and the girls keep him stocked with stolen goods in exchange for protection.

But it's not enough anymore. His list of charges is growing—possession of a firearm, robbery, intent to supply. He's deep in, and there's no way out.

That Friday, Jay sits in the public gallery at the Magistrates' Court, waiting for Tea Jay to be brought up from the cells for breaching bail.

"Fuck this, I've had enough," Jay thinks. "If he's remanded, I'll head back to Brum, face that dealer, and get myself on a methadone script. I can't do this anymore."

As Tea Jay is led into the courtroom, he catches sight of Jay in the gallery, their eyes locking for a brief moment.

As T.J. sits in the cell, his thoughts tangled between anger and despair. Jay—he was all he had left in the world. But it wasn't me protecting him, T.J. admits to himself. It was always Jay. Jay had the strength, the resilience, but T.J. had the skills—the knack for bringing in money, for making sure they survived.

They fed off each other's survival instincts, two broken halves of the same desperate whole. But now, sitting here, the thought gnaws at T.J.—what if Jay's out there, alone and spiralling? What if this time, I can't save him?

Six weeks later, Tea Jay sits on his bunk in prison, reading a letter from Frida. Jay is clean now, on a methadone script, trying to sort his life out. The words sting Tea Jay's heart as he's reminded of his own failure, his own inability to get clean.

Tears blur his vision, and he whispers to himself, "I can't live like this anymore. I've got to ask for real help."

Though locked away, Tea Jay is sober, at least from the substances that once consumed him. But the battle inside him rages on. He's still drowning in debt, his mind haunted by flashbacks and nightmares. The weight of his resentments and the chains of his past threaten to pull him under.

But in his darkest moment, he finds himself praying. And in that quiet, desperate act of surrender, he feels something he hasn't felt in years—a flicker of warmth, a tiny spark of hope.

Five months later, Tea Jay is standing in court for his drug treatment and testing order. He's clean, healthier than anyone remembers, and unrecognizable to the arresting officer who first brought him in.

The officer congratulates him, but adds a sombre warning: "I've seen people like you, Mr. Jay. They get clean, but they don't change. They don't grow. And two years later, they're dead. Don't be that guy."

Tea Jay brushes it off, his pride swelling. "I'm not like that. I've changed," he says confidently.

A month later, Tea Jay moves into a studio flat and starts attending fellowship meetings, where he meets Paula. She's kind, and the attention from her feels like a balm to his wounded ego. They grow close, and soon she offers him something more—a credit card in her name, with him as an additional cardholder.

"You have to promise to pay your part of the bill, though," she says nervously.

"Course I will," Tea Jay grins.

But months later, things unravel. Paula's furious. Tea Jay has maxed out her credit card, blowing past the £2,000 limit, and she demands to know where all the money went.

In his shame and desperation, Tea Jay hits the bar, drowning his sorrows. After ten months clean, he's back to square one. Worse, he's wanted for another GBH charge involving a guy from his treatment centre.

With nowhere else to turn, he jumps on a train back to the Midlands, hoping to outrun the mess he's made.

But years pass, and nothing changes. Tea Jay is stuck in a cycle of blame, a shadow of the man he could've been. He can't escape the past, the addiction, the self-destruction.

One evening, as he sits with friends and family, his heart shatters in an instant. The conversation turns to his childhood, to the abuse he endured. Just as he's about to speak, a voice cuts through the room—sharp, guilty.

"That was me."

VISION EXPRESS

"I'm so proud of you, Tea Jay. Look how far you've come. Your tests are tomorrow, right? You should be proud of yourself," his partner says, her voice filled with warmth.

"Hopefully, I'll pass," Tea Jay mumbles, though his nerves twist inside him.

"You will pass," she says with certainty.

"You've just read my mind!" he laughs, but the weight of tomorrow still hangs over him.

Feeling overwhelmed, he lies down to take a nap, hoping to shake off the day's stress. As he drifts off, the world around him starts to change.

Ahead, the road seems smooth at first, but obstacles rise up like shadows, threatening to stop him. An indescribable warmth surrounds him—loving, alive, protective. It's a comfort he's never known before, and yet, it feels strangely familiar.

Suddenly, he's sitting in a small church, surrounded by people who feel like old friends. Though he's never met them, they radiate acceptance. The happiness in the room is alien to him, but it wraps around him, filling the empty space inside.

This isn't just a dream, a voice whispers from within, a voice he's heard before.

You've been here before.

A sense of peace flows through him as words appear before his eyes:

I want you to stay here until I return to take you home.

You need to write it all down, Tea Jay. Write everything.

Suddenly, he's jolted awake by his partner's voice.

"Oi, Tea Jay! Wake up! You've pissed the bed again!" Lisa shouts, nudging him.

"What the...?" he mumbles, still half in his dream.

"It was all just a dream?" he says, blinking, trying to make sense of what just happened.

"You and your visions," Lisa laughs. "Where are my car keys?"

"Car keys? You don't even drive!" she teases, amused.

But Tea Jay shakes his head. "No, it can't have been a dream. It felt too real—more real than this."

"You're dreaming, mate," she chuckles. "You and your visions."

"Maybe. But it was so real... And on top of everything else, I stole shit loads of money from people, Lisa. I've had enough. I need to start trusting God. I need to sort myself out. I can't keep doing this. I need help," he confesses, his voice breaking.

Lisa, though sceptical, softens. "I've heard it all before, Tea Jay. Do you really mean it this time?"

This time, something in Tea Jay's eyes is different. "Yeah, this time I do."

As they sit together, Tea Jay suddenly feels the same electric warmth from his dream washing over him, just for an instant—enough to make him shiver.

Lisa, watching him closely, notices the change in his eyes. "What's going on with you? You look... different."

Tea Jay laughs, shaking his head, still trying to process everything. "I don't know, but I think I'm done with all this crap. I need to stop running."

Lisa crosses her arms, a soft smile tugging at her lips. "You've said that before, Tea Jay. But maybe this time is different."

"I'll prove it to you," he says with quiet determination.

Lisa studies him, her scepticism still there, but fading ever so slightly. "I hope you do, TJ. For your sake," she says, her voice soft but tinged with doubt.

TJ nods, feeling the weight of her words settle into his chest. As he watches her, that same electric warmth flickers through him again, like a silent promise deep in his soul. He can't explain it, but something feels different this time. It's not just the alcohol or the chaos driving him anymore—there's a spark inside, something growing, something more.

Lisa stands, pushing her hair behind her ear, her gaze lingering on TJ for a beat longer than usual. "You know... if you want to change, you've got to do more than just talk about it. I need to see it," she says, her voice almost pleading.

TJ swallows hard, determination flickering in his eyes. "You will."

For the first time in a long while, Lisa doesn't immediately brush him off. She simply watches him, unsure but hopeful, before quietly slipping out of the room.

As the door closes behind him, TJ stands still for a moment, letting the noise of the world blur around him. The hustle and bustle of the street feel distant, almost dreamlike, as though he's watching his life unfold from a distance. The weight of everything hangs in the air, thick and suffocating. He takes a deep breath, exhaling slowly, as if trying to purge the uncertainty clinging to his chest.

For the first time in years, something feels different. The warmth from earlier still pulses faintly in his veins, but now, it's mixed with something else—resolve. The familiar darkness whispers, but he pushes it aside, feeling it fight back. The thought lingers, heavy and undeniable: this is his last chance. If he doesn't change now, there may not be another moment like this. He tightens his fists, the weight of the world pressing on his shoulders, but for the first time in a long while, he believes he might be able to carry it.

THE PINK FLUFFY CLOUD

I t's been a few years since Lisa had enough and finally walked away, leaving Tea Jay alone in his spiralling chaos.

Tired of the way he's been living, Tea Jay stares at the selfie he's just taken—his face gaunt, his eyes hollow, and a heroin spliff hanging loosely from his mouth. His reflection reveals a man utterly lost. His clothes, which he's worn for weeks, are filthy, and the stench coming off him is unbearable. He hasn't showered in days. His tear-streaked face holds the unmistakable look of desperation. He's sick and tired of being sick and tired.

Determined to try something new, Tea Jay makes his way to an AA meeting, smelling to high heaven and dressed in rags. As he slips in quietly, hoping to go unnoticed, a man approaches him. "Are you new here?" he asks. Before Tea Jay can answer, he's introduced as a new-comer and welcomed warmly by the group, their kindness disarming him.

The smell of coffee and expensive cologne fills the air. One of the men places a mug of coffee in front of Tea Jay and a plate of biscuits. Starving, Tea Jay dives into the biscuits, barely waiting for his coffee.

His hands tremble—partly from the DTs, partly from the severe burns he suffered as a child—and the mug wobbles, spilling hot coffee onto his already scarred hand.

Despite the chaos in his life, there's a brief moment of peace. As he sits surrounded by strangers, Tea Jay breaks down, releasing a flood of tears he's kept bottled up for far too long. A member gently consoles him, offering support in a way that feels foreign, yet deeply needed.

Tea Jay sits, hunched and closed off, battling his inner demons. He wants to trust someone with the darkness of his past, but the weight of his nightmares—the beatings, the rape, the years of abuse—feels too heavy to share. No one here can know the real him. No one can know his shame.

No fuckin' way am I telling anyone here about my past. I just want to stop drinking, get clean, and maybe build a life with a decent job, a flat, and a girlfriend, Tea Jay tells himself.

As the meeting begins, Tea Jay is barely listening. His mind races with doubt and fear. But then, a man across the room says something that snaps him out of his haze: "Today can be your last drink, Tea Jay. It's the first one that does the damage."

The fuck's he talking about, 'the first one?' Tea Jay thinks. It's the eighth or ninth that got me nicked.

Someone else speaks up, adding with a smile, "No one's calling you an alcoholic here, Tea Jay, but I doubt you're here because you've eaten too many Mars bars."

Tea Jay can't help but chuckle at the absurdity of it all. But as he looks around the room, he suddenly feels a strange sense of déjà vu, as if he's been in this place before. He shakes it off as nonsense, but the feeling lingers.

The secretary offers him a chance to speak at the end of the meeting, but Tea Jay declines, saying he'll come back. He's handed a list of meetings and a few phone numbers. "Pick up the phone before you pick up a drink," one of the men advises.

Months pass, and Tea Jay's still sober. He starts taking better care of himself, attending an employment agency through the Jobcentre. His coach tells him he could earn free driving lessons or even an SIA security job license if he passes his exams. Excited, Tea Jay signs up, feeling a glimmer of hope.

But his aggressive tendencies remain. In the dry house where he's living, he picks a fight with a new resident over something trivial, threatening him with violence. When a support worker confronts him, Tea Jay lies, swearing he didn't make any threats. The guilt eats at him, but he's not ready to admit his failings.

"We had an appointment today, Tea Jay. You missed it again. Either sort your head out or find another sponsor," his sponsor says firmly over the phone.

"Sorry, mate," Tea Jay mutters, but he knows the truth. He's terrified of Step Four. No way I'm telling him what I've done. He'll judge me, laugh at me, or worse, he'll grass me up, Tea Jay thinks. What he doesn't know won't hurt him.

He goes through the motions, pretending to do the steps. When his sponsor asks if he's been honest, Tea Jay lies again, denying he's held anything back. But deep down, he knows he's only cheating himself.

Two weeks later, outside another dry house, Tea Jay finally confesses to his sponsor. "I lied. I didn't tell you the full truth. I got kicked out of the house for being aggressive. Then I drank. I wasn't honest in my Step Four."

His sponsor listens patiently before delivering a hard truth: "You'll get out of the steps what you put in, Tea Jay. You've been on a pink fluffy cloud for eleven months, but you haven't been living honestly. Recovery isn't just about staying sober—it's about changing your life. Until you do a proper Step Four and Five, until you take full responsibility for your actions, you'll always be sick. For us, drinking is death."

Tea Jay's sponsor's words cut deep. They linger in his mind, a harsh reminder that sobriety isn't just about abstaining from substances—it's about confronting the truth, no matter how painful.

ACCEPTANCE IS THE ANSWER

Desperately in need of forgiveness and reassurance, Tea Jay kneels on the living room floor, utterly beaten, broken, and bewildered. His mind is swirling with regret, and his heart is heavy. Tears stream down his blood-red face, soaking the carpet beneath him as he opens his arms in a plea for help. He is lost, a man crushed under the weight of his past choices, yearning for some form of peace.

He closes his eyes and calls out to his higher power, Jesus Christ, the only force he believes can pull him out of the darkness he's been living in. I can't do this on my own, his soul cries out in silent desperation.

Suddenly, a surge of warmth flows through him, from the crown of his head down into his heart. The sensation is electric—alive—and it brings an immediate sense of calm to his troubled spirit. As he continues to pray, his sobs quiet, and he loses himself in the moment. The energy envelops him, and for a brief moment, the negative voices in his mind fade, replaced by a feeling of acceptance he has never known before.

He wants to change. He can feel it deep inside his soul—a remorseful yearning to alter the course of his life. His spirit is tired of fighting, of running, and of hiding from the truth. I need help, he admits, finally ready to surrender.

Tea Jay recites the sinner's prayer again, but this time it feels different. This time, he means it.

What the hell's going to be different this time? a voice in his mind sneers, trying to undermine his resolve. He's heard this voice before—it's the enemy within, trying to keep him in chains.

Yet, even as doubt creeps in, another wave of warmth flows through him, bringing with it a deeper peace. It's as if his very soul is being bathed in an ocean of love, washing away years of anger, guilt, and shame.

In that moment, Tea Jay feels a message pierce his heart, a thought not his own, but one that feels intensely personal: Although I forgive you, my child, it will take time for you to forgive yourself. Write a letter to your brothers and sisters, Tea Jay. Your words will reach many, but there's one heart in particular that needs your message.

The sensation of love intensifies, and Tea Jay is overwhelmed by the emotion flooding his heart. He recalls hearing this same voice twice before—once after he was viciously attacked and assaulted, and again when he nearly died in a hospital in Bristol.

What does your heart tell you, Tea Jay? the voice asks again, gentler this time.

To write a book, Tea Jay thinks, almost instinctively.

At that very moment, another wave of energy, like pure love, pierces his heart, igniting a fire within him. The voice resounds once more: Acceptance, Tea Jay. That's the answer to all your problems.

Acceptance? Tea Jay questions, unsure of the meaning.

That's right. Acceptance is the key. You'll find your answers in the heart, but you must have faith.

For a moment, Tea Jay feels a reverence, a sense of awe and wonder at the experience. But then, almost reflexively, he laughs, still caught between belief and disbelief.

Tea Jay is living in a privately rented flat in the Midlands, an old building with more problems than he can handle. The flat is in a rundown neighbourhood, and his past seems to haunt every corner. To get to his flat, you have to pass through a short alleyway and climb a set of steep rickety steps. His neighbours downstairs are just as shady as the flat itself, stealing his post from the external mailbox and applying for credit in his name.

The property itself is a mess. A small kitchen greets you at the entrance, its black electric cooker broken and the cold, ripped grey lino peeling away from the floor. The walls are drab, and the hallway that connects the kitchen to the living room is dark, with nothing but a filthy industrial carpet covering the floor.

In the living room, there's an air of discomfort. The walls are painted a dull mocha, and the furnishings are mismatched—a leather two-seater on one side and a three-seater opposite. The windows are covered by coffee-coloured curtains, and a 55-inch television sits in the far corner. The floorboards creak ominously, with holes in the wood where small creatures frequently scurry, much to the horror of Tea Jay's girlfriend.

"What was that...?" she screams, her voice panicked.

"It's a tarantula," Tea Jay jokes, though his laugh is hollow.

"It's only a bleeding mouse," Tea Jay goes on to reassure her.

It's now Monday, two days after Tea Jay's spiritual experience. He accepts that he can't do this on his own and calls his previous sponsor, asking for help.

"Good to hear from you, Tea Jay! Have you had enough pain, and are you willing to go to any lengths and accept life on life's terms?"

Tea Jay admits that he's willing, but he's also wrapped in fear. He's terrified someone will find his personal inventory and use it against him. However, something within tells him that it's best to take those risks and trust someone, or he'll no doubt drink again. And for him, drinking means death.

His sponsor reassures him that this fear is normal. He reminds Tea Jay that most people worry about others thinking about them when, in reality, most people are thinking about themselves.

"Why are you projecting and worrying about Step Four? Step Four is for another day. You haven't even done Step One yet. So, live in today," his sponsor laughs.

He continues, suggesting Tea Jay get involved in service in AA and sets him a task:

"I want you to write three examples of how you are powerless over alcohol. Each example should take up a side of A4 paper. Then, write three examples of how your life has become unmanageable, again on three sides of A4. You've got a week to do it."

"How come I still feel like shit inside?" Tea Jay asks.

"Because, although you've made the most important step by asking for help, you're only just beginning your journey. Besides, there's a little boy inside of you that needs a lot of nurturing, and that will take time," his sponsor replies.

"All these are only suggestions, Tea Jay. But let me ask you this: if you were in an airplane that was going to crash and the pilot suggested you put on a parachute, would you do it? You'd do it because the parachute would save your life. Well, going through the steps and being willing to go to any lengths is your parachute—it will save your life."

"That makes sense," Tea Jay says, feeling the weight of the conversation settle on him.

After completing Steps One, Two, and Three, it's time for the step Tea Jay has dreaded most—Step Four. The inventory. The step where he must write down his resentments, the harm he has done, his fears, and his conduct with others.

He sits down to write, terrified of facing his inner demons. But he knows this is a life-or-death task, and he needs to take it seriously. For each resentment, he lists the name of the person he resents, the cause of that resentment, and how it affects him. He writes:

I'm resentful at:

The cause: (Explain what happened)

Affects my: (List what part of you is affected—self-esteem, pride, security, etc.)

Example:

I'm resentful at: Mr. Smith

The cause: He tried to make a move on my girlfriend.

Affects my: Self-esteem, sex relations, and pride. (Fear of losing her)

Tea Jay goes on, page after page, listing every single person, situation, and fear that has weighed him down throughout his life. It's brutal, but it's necessary. For every resentment, he asks himself, "What's my part in it?" forcing himself to take ownership of his actions.

Then comes the harms he's done to others:

I harmed:

The harm done: (Describe the harm)

My part in it: (Explain why you did it)

Example:

I harmed: Mr. Smith

The harm done: I attacked him when I was drunk.

My part in it: I was jealous and paranoid about him being with my girlfriend.

He includes everything, from physical harm to financial harm, and even emotional manipulation. Nothing is left unexamined. Over the course of a month, Tea Jay writes more than 200 pages, pouring out the darkest corners of his soul.

After finishing Step Four, he goes to his sponsor for Step Five—confession. He reads everything aloud, every ugly detail, to his sponsor. It's exhausting, but as he speaks, he feels the weight beginning to lift. He's unburdening himself, finally confronting the things that have haunted him.

When they finish, his sponsor reminds him that the goal is not just to confess but to make amends. Tea Jay must now prepare for Steps Eight and Nine, where he'll reach out to those he has harmed and seek their forgiveness. But before that, he takes Steps Six and Seven, asking his Higher Power to remove his character defects.

It's a long process, but as the days go on, Tea Jay feels lighter. His mind, once clouded with guilt and shame, starts to clear. He begins making amends where he can, though some debts are harder to repay than others.

In the meantime, Tea Jay starts doing service in AA. He also volunteers at a local charity shop, finding solace in doing something good for others. Slowly, his self-esteem begins to rebuild, not through grand gestures, but through the simple act of helping where he can.

As Tea Jay navigates his recovery, he faces a painful personal reality. His mother, Elizabeth, has been suffering from vascular memory impairment due to years of alcohol abuse, and now it's progressed to full vascular dementia. She's been in a nursing home for a few years now.

The nursing home is small but warm, and Tea Jay visits her regularly. As he enters her room, he's greeted by family photos and memories of a lifelong past.

"How come you're trying to stop me smoking, piss-ant?" Elizabeth snaps, her confusion evident.

"Mom, I'm not trying to stop you from smoking. Look, I brought you forty fags! I'll give them to the carers," Tea Jay replies gently.

"Piss off! Give them here. I don't trust those robbing cows!" she snaps again.

"Why hasn't Jay been to see me?" she asks, looking confused.

"He came up yesterday, Mom," Tea Jay lies, knowing that the truth would break her heart.

Tea Jay knows his mother's illness means she can't remember what's real anymore. But he doesn't want to upset her, so he just smiles, kisses her on the forehead, and says goodbye.

Outside, Tea Jay tells his sister Lacey, "It didn't half put me in a predicament, lying to Mom about Jay. It'd kill her if she finds out what's happened to him."

Lacey, TJ's sister, has always been a fighter, but it's her heart that makes her extraordinary. As the smallest in the family, life has thrown every storm her way, yet she stands firm, her love unshakable. Even in the worst moments, when their mother's memory fades and Jay's absence gnaws at them, Lacey's spirit remains a beacon of hope. She carries the weight of the family, always smiling for her children, always loving, even when it feels like there's nothing left to give. And in this moment, as TJ looks into her eyes, he feels a wave of gratitude so deep it steals his breath. How did she become the strongest of them all? How did she survive where he crumbled? She's everything he wishes he could be, and he loves her with a fierceness that makes his chest ache.

Outside, TJ repeats to his sister, "Didn't know I'd put myself in this predicament, lying to mum about Jay, but it'll kill her if she finds out what's happened to him."

Lacey, though weighed down by the same pain, stands as always—strong, unwavering. "We'll get through this," she whispers, but even her voice, steady as it is, carries the cracks of all they've lost. TJ glances at her, feeling a lump form in his throat, knowing that while he might be crumbling inside, she remains the glue holding their world together. For once, he wishes he could be half the strength she is.

GIVING RATHER THAN GETTING

It's been suggested by his sponsor that Tea Jay read at least four pages each day from the Big Book and live just one day at a time. It's also recommended that he pray every morning, asking for a sober day, and say thank you at night before going to bed.

Tea Jay writes a gratitude list and refers to it whenever he feels fed up. Deep down, he knows he can't stay sober on his own. He doesn't just want God in his life—he accepts that he needs a conscious relationship with Him. For Tea Jay, that means connecting with God.

Although Tea Jay spends at least forty-five minutes each morning in prayer and meditation, reading his New Life Recovery Bible, The Big Book, and Daily Reflections, he still struggles with his mental health. Intrusive thoughts continue to plague him, and he often loses his temper around his loved ones. However, he recognizes that after thirty years of alcohol and drug use, these thoughts won't disappear overnight.

Recently, his mental health team increased his Pregabalin to morning and evening doses to help manage his moods, alongside a higher dose of antipsychotic medication. But Tea Jay has started to accept that a lot of his anger comes down to choice and self-control. He reminds himself of four key questions whenever he feels the urge to speak out of anger:

1. Does it need to be said?
2. Does it need to be said by me?
3. What do I hope to gain from saying this?
4. Should I run this by my sponsor before saying it?

For some reason, Tea Jay finds it easier to let go of bigger problems than the small, everyday annoyances. But he's grateful to have a good sponsor and the ability to pick up the phone before picking up a drink.

Tea Jay often struggles with negative thoughts from his past, making it difficult for him to connect with others. Even in AA, where everyone shares a common goal, Tea Jay still feels like a square peg in a round hole. He tends to keep to himself, finding more comfort in being alone, except when he's with his girlfriend or family.

He's also been experiencing déjà vu, with recurring memories of someone or something showing him visions or dreams where he faces numerous obstacles before writing a book. The first time he had this vision, he was with his ex, Lisa, and couldn't even read or write properly. Despite having such low self-esteem, he never believed he'd pass his basic exams.

Recently, Tea Jay has taken pride in passing his driving test, earning the incentive of twenty free driving lessons after completing his English, Maths, and I.T. GCSEs while in his forties. Now, he drives a new Nissan Qashqai in a nightshade colour, feeling a sense of accomplishment.

Six months into his voluntary role at a charity shop, Tea Jay enjoys the work even more than his paid jobs. He feels a sense of purpose, working alongside his colleagues and engaging in banter. However, the deep-rooted feelings of not belonging persist, though he knows they will eventually fade with time.

He's also taken on service roles within AA and has fully joined the fellowship, no longer just attending meetings. Approaching twelve months sober, Tea Jay hears on the news about a virus outbreak in Wuhan, China, but thinks little of it. He and his partner even book a five-day holiday to Malaga.

Once they land in Malaga, Tea Jay feels the familiar compulsion to drink. It's hot, they're on holiday, and he thinks to himself, "Who'll know if I take a drink?"

His conscience kicks in: "You would know, you loon!" With a shudder, Tea Jay picks up the phone and calls his sponsor, who congratulates him for reaching out before picking up a drink.

"Well done for calling me first! Remember, if you get a good idea, call me. If you get a great idea, come find me!" his sponsor laughs.

Tea Jay reflects, "Our ideas as alcoholics, especially early in recovery, seem great in our heads, but they're not always clever in reality."

After returning from Malaga in March, Tea Jay and his partner head straight to the care home to visit his mother. But the carers eye them warily, knowing they've just come from Spain, which has become a red-light country for travellers due to the COVID-19 outbreak.

"The UK's just gone into lockdown," Tea Jay tells his partner.

"Oh my God, we only got back yesterday! If we'd flown back today, we wouldn't have been allowed to!" she replies.

"You'd better call your son because it looks like you'll be living with me for the time being," Tea Jay adds.

Two weeks later, Tea Jay and his partner begin to show flu-like symptoms. However, the symptoms aren't the typical high fever and cough associated with COVID-19.

"I don't feel well. I'm so tired, I ache all over, and I can't breathe properly, Tea Jay," his partner says, panicking.

Although both are diagnosed with COVID-19, his partner recovers after two weeks. But Tea Jay's condition worsens, and he suffers from panic attacks. Fearing for his life, he finally calls an ambulance.

UNCONDITIONAL LOVE

F orgiveness isn't something that should only be given when it's
deserved, nor should it be handed out just to release feelings
of resentment or vengeance towards someone who has harmed you.
Forgiveness means different things to different people, but in its truest
form, it should be given unconditionally.

Although forgiveness often means choosing to let go of the anger
tied to a hurtful event, for people like Tea Jay, dealing with and accepting the original pain and difficult memories is another challenge
entirely. Memories that might never truly disappear.

Forgiveness doesn't rebuild a relationship—it's about freeing yourself and the person you hold anger towards. Letting go. It's an unconditional release from the harmful intentions, thoughts, or reminders
of the harm caused. It's freedom from fear, and the opportunity to
move forward.

The pain often comes from avoidance—avoiding the very issues
that shouldn't be avoided.

In Tea Jay's case, much of his pain stemmed from never asking for
help during his adolescence. As he grew into adulthood, he contin-

ually searched for pain by seeking answers, searching for someone to
blame, instead of searching for ways to forgive.

Take his burning accident as an example: Tea Jay often wonders,
who truly scalded his hand? Was it his birth mother or the foster
mother? But does it really matter who did it?

Realistically, continuing to search for someone to point the finger
at, rather than seeking forgiveness, makes it all about himself, doesn't
it?

Blame

Blame: Now, draw a line with a ruler between the letters A and M.
What does it say?

Blame becomes: Bla, bla, bla... me, me, me.

When Tea Jay reflects on this, he realizes that the act of continually
searching for answers is nothing more than a way to manufacture
more pain and fuel self-centeredness.

Whether it was his birth mother or foster mother who caused the
injury, the act of forgiveness, being unconditional by nature, means it
doesn't matter who was responsible. What matters is the release.

Another example comes from alcoholism and mental illness. There
might be some justification for forgiving someone whose actions were
shaped by their alcoholism or mental health struggles. Alcoholism,
after all, is both a physical, mental, and spiritual illness that warps the
mind and ravages the body.

The Big Book of Alcoholics Anonymous highlights this in The
Doctor's Opinion, pages xxv to xxxii of the fourth edition. It's clear
that alcoholics don't always understand the damage they cause. Their
illness blinds them.

Would you judge someone with dementia for making mistakes?
Likely not. Then, why judge someone whose mind has been equally
compromised by addiction?

The answer seems simple, but it's one Tea Jay has wrestled with for years. His own mother, Elizabeth, suffers from vascular dementia, a condition that was accelerated by years of alcohol abuse. She, like many others, made choices under the influence of a disease that clouded her judgment.

Elizabeth was one of four children born shortly after the second world war. Bright and full of promise, she excelled in school, surrounded by friends. But she married young and fell in love quickly, with a man who left her broken hearted. Always in the background, though, was Jimmy B, the Irishman who seemed to take centre stage as Elizabeth's marriage began to unravel.

When her marriage dissolved, she turned to Jimmy Beam—her nickname for the drink that became her crutch. Yet, even though the darkest times, she ensured her children never went without. They always had food on the table, clothes on their backs, and they never missed out on holidays.

Lacey fondly remembers their mother's entrepreneurial spirit. "Mom always knew how to make a few quid," Lacey laughs to her husband. "Do you remember all the tobacco and gammon she used to sell?"

Her husband chuckles. "Yep, always a hustle going on with Liz."

"Got any tobacco or fags for sale, Liz?" a neighbour would ask.

"How many packets do you want?" Liz would reply with a smirk. "I've got some eggs and gammon too, if you're interested."

It wasn't just survival. For Liz, it was about ensuring her kids never felt abandoned, even when their father left them with nothing. She always found a way to make ends meet.

Even as Elizabeth's health deteriorates and dementia tightens its grip, Tea Jay reflects on his mother's legacy—her resilience, her drive, and the love that, despite everything, never faltered. Memories of her hustle, her sharp tongue, and her trips to visit friends, like her school-mate Patty in Canada, still bring smiles.

Tea Jay chuckles as he recalls the story. "You've got a lot of money there, little lady," an American customs officer had remarked to Elizabeth during one of her trips abroad.

"Yeah... to spend in your bloody country, you cheeky cowbag!" Elizabeth had snapped, her fiery spirit never dulled.

"Well, Liz, welcome to our border force." Patty laughs, hugging her old school friend.

"Remember when I took Mom to Dublin, sis?" Tea Jay laughs.

"Hold on to your handbags, girls. This is the closest you're ever going to get to an orgasm," Elizabeth shouts just as the plane takes off, sitting next to a Catholic priest who bursts out laughing.

"Mom's having to move to another care home in Shirley because Birds Hill can't handle her," Lacey says to Tea Jay over the phone.

"Remember pushing Mom down that hill at Hatton Locks?" Tea Jay sniggers to his fiancée.

"Ahh, I want to get out, you bastard!" Elizabeth shouts as her son pushes her faster in her wheelchair down the locks.

"That's a good way to get rid of her," a passerby jokes, laughing as Tea Jay speeds along with the wheelchair by the canal.

"I've just got the insurance out on her," Tea Jay quips, laughing along with the passerby.

Hatton Locks is where Tea Jay and his fiancée went on their first date. A picturesque canal runs through the little town of Hatton in the Warwickshire countryside, with locks as far as the eye can see, leading towards Warwick. There's also a quaint little canal-side café with outdoor seating, just off the A4177 into Hatton Village. The Hatton Lock's restaurant serves beautiful, five-star food at very reasonable prices, making it a comfortable, scenic spot for a meal.

"Mom won't eat or drink, and she's sleeping most of the time," Lacey says, tears in her eyes.

"She's had a lot of pain in her life, but she's had a hell of a lot of love from us kids and her grandkids, who absolutely adore her," Tea Jay replies.

"She's still alert," Lacey adds, trying to reassure herself.

"Mom, do you believe in God?" Tea Jay asks gently.

"Of course I do. He's always with me," Elizabeth smiles, her voice soft.

"Would you like to give your life to Him? We can all say it together right now," Tea Jay says, tears streaming down his cheeks.

"Okay," Elizabeth agrees.

Hello there...

I bet this is a surprise. Yes, I'm talking to you—the one who's been following this story all the way through. I know you've been reading closely, so let's not pretend otherwise

You've obviously felt at home here, maybe even seen parts of your own story. I'd love to invite you to join us as we pray for our mother. No pressure—you're not being asked to give your life to God, unless you feel moved to. But it would mean a lot if you simply joined us in prayer.

Giving your life to a higher power isn't about following a set of rules or going to church every week. It's about living a spiritual life and turning your will—your thinking—and your life—your actions—over to the care of God daily. This is deeply personal and entirely your choice.

Is everyone ready?

Just repeat these words within your heart:

Father God, I repent of my sins and surrender my life to you. Please wash me clean. I believe that you are the Son of God, that you died on the cross for my sins, and rose again from the dead on the third day. I believe in my heart and confess with my mouth that you alone are my Lord and Saviour. Amen.

It's now the following week, and when Tea Jay enters his mother's room at the care home, she's laughing with someone, saying, "Put me back up there; I don't want to stay here. Eh, put me bleeding back, you."

"Who're you talking to, Mom?" Tea Jay giggles, glancing up at the ceiling where she's looking.

"I'm talking to them up there," she says, chuckling.

Two days later, on Friday, Tea Jay's fiancée hands him the phone.

"We're at the hospital with Mom. They've told us all to be here with her," Lacey's husband says.

"Aren't they worried about Covid restrictions?" Tea Jay asks suspiciously.

"Be as quick as you can," Lacey's husband replies, his voice heavy.

As Tea Jay races to the hospital, tears soaking his face, he regrets all the times he blamed his mother for the past.

There's an overwhelming sense of misery, pain, and fear at the hospital. The atmosphere is icy and unapproachable. Though the casualty ward is bustling with activity, there's a deadly silence around Tea Jay and his loved ones.

All he wants now is to see his mother's smiling eyes one last time. He realises at this moment that life is too short for regrets.

"She's got sepsis, and they've told us she may not last the night," Lacey says, her tears streaming down her face.

Their mother's breathing is shallow under the oxygen mask, her eyes fixed, staring ahead.

"Do you mind if we all pray?" Tea Jay asks softly.

"Of course not," Lacey whispers through her tears.

Under tear-soaked faces, everyone bows their heads as Tea Jay leads them in prayer.

As Tea Jay bows his head to pray, he feels the weight of the past lifting, replaced by a deep sense of love and forgiveness. For the first time in his life, he feels a powerful connection to his family—a bond that transcends the pain, the mistakes, and the misunderstandings. In this moment, surrounded by those who have shared his journey, he knows that love is the thread that holds them all together. It isn't perfect, and neither is forgiveness, but it's real. And for Tea Jay, that's enough.

WHAT'S THE DIFFERENCE

Tea Jay shivers as a sudden flash of his past negative voice resurfaces, trying to shove the flood of flashbacks to the back of his mind.

The buzz Tea Jay feels from outsmarting the system fills him with twisted satisfaction. The system, in his eyes, threw him to the dogs, leaving him worthless.

But deep down, it's all self-pity and bitterness. He refuses to acknowledge the truth: this is vengeance, and beneath it all is fear, hiding behind a mask of strength.

"So fuckin' what?" Tea Jay snaps, his voice sharp, defensive.

"Why are you so angry?" the prison officer asks, calm and measured.

"Tch, what the fuck do you care?" Tea Jay fires back, his eyes narrowing.

"Oh, I get it—you think I'm just another cog in the system, part of the establishment?" The officer's tone is calm, unfazed by Tea Jay's outburst.

"You think you know me? You don't know jack shit," Tea Jay rants, his anger rising, pushing everyone away.

The question lingers, softer now, echoing in his mind: "Why are you so angry?"

Tea Jay has heard it countless times—from prison officers, social workers, family members, counsellors. And every time, his answer is the same.

"Listen, guv, if you'd been through half the shit I've been through, you'd be just like me," Tea Jay says defensively.

"Does it matter what you've been through? You're alive, breathing, and you have the power to make choices. But until you start accepting what's happened, you'll keep stumbling toward a lonely, miserable end," the officer says, his voice firm yet compassionate. "Blame is a choice when you're too scared to face the person in the mirror. Are you a coward, Tea Jay?"

"I'm no fuckin' coward," Tea Jay snaps, defences up.

"There it is again—'I'm no fuckin' coward,'" the officer replies. "That's fear talking, Tea Jay. All that anger... it's fear."

"Tch, what do you mean by that?" Tea Jay asks sarcastically, though his voice shakes beneath the surface.

"Why is everything about you?" the officer asks, watching him closely.

"If you'd lived my life, you'd drink, steal, and think, 'fuck 'em all' too," Tea Jay mutters, voice hard, but the uncertainty in his eyes betrays him.

The officer meets his gaze, unwavering. "How do you know I haven't been through worse than you?"

Tea Jay looks at him, startled. "Have ya?"

"I might have," the officer says, his expression unreadable.

"How'd you get to where you are now?" Tea Jay asks, curiosity mixing with disbelief.

"I let go of myself. I asked for help," the officer says simply.

Later, Tea Jay reflects on this. One of the screws said he was a recovering alcoholic... Maybe there's hope for me yet. Really? Who am I trying to kid? he thinks.

A familiar voice, steady and calm, whispers within. You'll need more than words to change, Tea Jay. It's going to take time and patience. But change is possible.

"What the...? Where did that come from?" Tea Jay mutters, shaken by the clarity of the inner voice.

You know exactly where it came from, and who's speaking to you, Tea Jay, the voice says gently. You've prayed to me for years, and my answer has always been yes. But I'll only ever do for you that you cannot do for yourself.

"I can't believe how many excuses I used to make, just to avoid facing reality. I lived in a place called Blame for years—bla, bla, bla, me, me, me," Tea Jay reflects, his heart heavy with the realisation.

When Tea Jay begins to accept through his faith in his higher power and the AA programme that he isn't alone, he starts to see things differently. He accepts that he has an illness, and it's not just about alcohol or drugs. The real problem, he realises, is himself.

The substances were only ever the solution to numb his deeper pain. But now, with the tools of recovery, he knows the solution is within himself, if he's willing to face it.

Of course, testing days will come. There will always be struggles—after all, we are only as good as we are today. But through self-sacrifice, accepting life on life's terms, and remaining teachable, Tea Jay knows he can make it. Living in the solution, not the problem, is his only path forward.

Through the guidance of his sponsor and the humility of practicing the twelve steps, Tea Jay identifies his defects of character. He knows now that the only way to face these demons is to conduct a thorough personal inventory through an honest and brutal Step Four. But first, he has to complete the first three steps and fully grasp the foundation of the programme.

So, what's the difference today?

The difference is change—demonstrated through humility, self-reflection, and the willingness to accept help. The difference is Tea Jay no longer lives in a world where blame is his compass. Instead, he's learning to take responsibility, to seek out his defects, and to commit to change, one day at a time.

For Tea Jay, the only way he could accept his powerlessness was to look at not just alcohol but to look at what any other substances did to him once they passed his lips or went into his veins. He had, and indeed still has, to painfully accept and admit, just one day at a time, that he has absolutely no power whatsoever over what those substances will do to him once they're in his system.

The second part of Step One says that his life, once he's taken a drink or substance, becomes unmanageable. You only have to look at his homelessness, the police cells, the debts, the prison sentences, and the partners he drank away—including his ex-wife. And then there's the family he's hurt, not forgetting the near-death experiences. All of this shows how unmanageable his life was.

Tea Jay knows the only way he can stay sober, just one day at a time, is to accept completely that he cannot take a drink or drug. All the steps are important for maintaining a balanced life and ongoing sobriety, but Step One is the most crucial. Without Step One, people like Tea Jay don't survive.

"Hello, my name's Tea Jay, and I'm a very grateful recovering alcoholic and addict.

How do I practice Step One every day? It starts with some vital disciplines every morning. First, I don't just pray and ask for a sober day. I have to build a relationship with God by being willing to listen and change.

How do I do that? Well, I get on my knees out of respect and reverence, and I say the Lord's Prayer. I invite my higher power into my heart and focus on the areas of my life that need work. I ask for His strength and His blessings to help me change. But I also have to be willing to listen.

You might ask, 'How do I listen to God?'

Well, God is like a parent. If I'm selfish in my asking, what do you think He's going to say? So, I have to be willing to accept the answers, even if they come over time. There's such a thing as 'no' or 'yes, but not right now.' This teaches me patience and keeps me teachable.

Every day, I read at least four pages of my Big Book, my Daily Reflections, and a chapter from my True-Life Recovery Bible. And I just don't drink in between. I start in the Big Book from page xi and go to page 164, then I start again. I never get bored of it because, as I grow and learn, I always get a different message.

These disciplines take me about half an hour to an hour in the morning. If I have something planned, I get up earlier. My sobriety comes first because, whatever I put before my recovery, I'll lose.

Step Two says: 'We came to believe that a Power greater than ourselves could restore us to sanity.' Even though I have faith now, I can't forget how insane my life was. I desperately needed that higher power to restore me to sanity.

If I had to define insanity, it would be taking a drink or drug after a period of sobriety and expecting a different result.

Step Three says: 'We made a decision to turn our will and our lives over to the care of God as we understood Him.' I've made plenty of decisions in my life, but nothing changed until I turned my will—my thinking—and my life—my actions—over to God.

I could only truly accept this step after completing Step Four, which I've talked about before. But let me give you another example.

I had to list all my resentments, breaking them down: Who? Why? What was affected—pride, ego, self-esteem? What was I afraid of? Was it places I resented? Was there guilt over my behaviour there?

1. I had to list all my resentments.

2. I had to list all the harms I caused.

3. I had to list all my conduct in relationships, especially when drinking—lying, stealing money, disappearing for days.

4. I had to list all my fears and intrusive thoughts, then share them with my sponsor in Step Five.

Step Five says: 'Admitted to God, to ourselves, and to another human being the exact nature of our wrongs.'

Trusting someone wasn't easy at first, especially with my fear of being judged. But I knew it was the only way to start healing.

I tried to hide certain areas of my life from my sponsor originally. But this is a program of action—it's about brutal honesty and humility. There's no such thing as a "little bit of dishonesty, and as a result of my initial dishonesty, I ended up drinking again.

And for an alcoholic, to drink is to die.

So, I had to get honest.

Funny enough, when I finally told my sponsor the things I'd been hiding, he just laughed and said, "Is that all?"

I remember thinking, do you know the turmoil and fear I've gone through over this? And then I just laughed at myself.

Step Six says:

We were entirely ready to have God remove all these defects of character.

Step Six for me is all about being willing to change. Doing a moral inventory and sharing it with your sponsor is one thing. But being willing to actually change—to amend your ways and attitudes—is something totally different.

But it's what saves your life.

Step Seven says:

Humbly asked Him to remove our shortcomings.

These two steps, Steps Six and Seven, separate the men from the boys, and the women from the girls. Asking humbly, for me, means staying teachable and consistently working on the behaviours and issues that demand attention in order to truly change.

Step Eight says:

Made a list of all persons we had harmed and became willing to make amends to them all.

What do you think?

Yes, I'm talking to you again, the one who's reading this right now. What does it mean to "become willing"?

I compiled my Step Eight list of amends from my Step Four inventory.

Step Nine says:

Made direct amends to such people wherever possible, except when to do so would injure them or others.

For me, Step Nine is all about humility and demonstrating real change. It's not about me—it's about the other person.

The second part of Step Nine is crucial:

Except when to do so would injure them or others.

Some harms couldn't be made face-to-face. In some cases, my Step Nine amends were financial, donating to a charity in the name of the person I had harmed.

One valuable lesson I've learned is that Step Nine isn't about me; it's about making it right for the other person.

Step Ten says:

Continued to take personal inventory, and when we were wrong, promptly admitted it.

I'm only as good as I am today. I haven't had a character transplant. If I'm wrong, I apologize—and most importantly, I take action to amend my behaviour.

Step Eleven says:

Sought through prayer and meditation to improve our conscious contact with God as we understood Him, praying only for knowledge of His will for us and the power to carry it out.

As I mentioned earlier, the steps aren't something you just work through once and then move on. Step eleven, like all the others, is about gaining and maintaining a relationship with God by continuously applying them to your life.

What was that you just said? Yes, I'm talking to you again—the one who's reading this right now, the one who's listening as I go on and on.

Just for the record, whenever I mention God, I'm talking about your own conception of God. Whatever you choose to believe in, whatever works for you—it's about the God of your understanding.

God? Why should I trust in God? What has He ever done for me? I hear you cry out.

Let me answer that with the simplest response I can—Hello, you're breathing, aren't you? I know there's more to it than that. Maybe you're wondering...

Why is there so much suffering in the world? Why are there always wars?

By man's just, is by his faith.

God didn't create the world's problems—man did. And until we put things right, those problems will either stay the same or get worse, spiralling out of control.

Why do people die so young for no reason?

You're probably wondering. There's always a bigger picture at play—one we may not always see. Who are we to question God's plan unless, of course, you know what it is?

God is infallible—meaning, He's perfect. He sent His son, to die for us all. If you need proof, look into near-death experiences (NDEs). There are countless stories online—testimonies from those who've crossed over and returned. Or check out true stories like Heaven is for Real or Miracles from Heaven. They're living proof of God's hand in everything.

I've died three times, and each time I survived because God has a purpose for my life. He has a purpose for yours, too. One of mine, I believe, is passing this message on to you. What you do with it is entirely up to you—it's your choice.

Hello I'm talking to you again. Yes you, the one reading this right now. Are you ready to surrender and to embrace change?

You can't buy compassion, love, selflessness, or humility. These are blessings that God gives freely to the humble, the lost, and the peacemakers.

God freed me from my prison of addiction, alcoholism, debt, loneliness, gluttony, and fear. He brought me—and many others—into a higher existence filled with love, peace, and hope.

Step twelve says:

Having had a spiritual awakening as a result of these steps, we tried to carry this message to alcoholics and practice these principles in all our affairs.

But this isn't just for alcoholics, addicts, or gamblers. Don't think you're off the hook.

This could about you—the one reading this right now.

Do you think you're just hearing about someone who had it rough? Well, you'd be very wrong.

Please, just between you and me, take a moment to reflect on your life and personalise these steps for yourself.

If you're ready and willing, walk through the steps. Start with step one and be honest about what needs changing. Then, do a step four and share it with a trusted spiritual advisor, a priest, or a good friend who can keep their mouths shut. Just remember, it can't be your spouse or parents—it's got to be someone unaffected by what you share.

The rule is simple:

You have to be hard on yourself, but always considerate of others. We have no right to save our own skin at the expense of someone else's.

This book isn't just about me; it's about you too.

If you feel there's something in you that needs changing, go back to step one. Identify the areas where you're powerless and where your life has become unmanageable. We'll work through it together it together, I promise. And if you're wondering, we'll get into more of it very soon.

SORRY ISN'T ENOUGH

T J sits at the edge of the table, fingers tracing the rim of a coffee cup, his mind swirling with the weight of words unspoken. The silence in the room is thick, hanging between him and the person across from him—someone he's hurt more times than he can count. Years of drunkenness have made him reckless with apologies, throwing "sorry" out like a lifeline when all it ever did was sink under the weight of his actions.

But today feels different. There's no whisky fog clouding his mind, no slurred words or empty promises. He's sober, fully present, and the word "sorry" sticks in his throat like a stone he can't swallow. It's too easy, too small for the damage he's done.

He opens his mouth to speak, to say what he's always said. "I'm sorry."

The words fall flat, hollow, like they always do. He knows it, and more importantly, the person sitting across from him knows it. Their eyes meet his, not with anger this time, but with something worse—indifference. It's as if every sorry he's ever uttered has built a wall between them, one so thick that not even his sobriety can tear it down.

TJ clenches his fists under the table, frustration boiling in his chest. Sobriety is supposed to fix things, isn't it? Isn't this the part where people forgive him, where the healing starts?

But sorry isn't enough. It never was.

TJ remembers the first time the word "sorry" started to lose its meaning. It was the fire. A young boy, curious and careless, he accidentally set fire to the house. When the flames were doused and the smoke cleared, he confessed the truth. But by then, it was too late. His family looked at him with disbelief. Sorry? What could sorry possibly fix? The damage was already done, and once again, words were not enough to undo the mess he had made.

Years later, it happened again. He was six or seven, accused of stealing something at school—a crime he didn't commit, but one he took the blame for out of fear. The teacher was harsh, her voice thundered with authority, and in that moment, the lie felt like the only way to escape her wrath.

When he got home, he told his mum the truth. "I didn't do it," he said, tears streaming down his face. But the damage had already been done. His first lie, spoken out of fear, and the word "sorry" that followed meant nothing. His mum didn't believe him. And why should she? He had already broken the fragile trust that existed between them. That's when he first understood—sometimes, sorry isn't enough.

By the time TJ turned 17, the word "sorry" had become just that—a word. One he used more out of habit than sincerity. It was his shield, the thing he threw out whenever his actions left destruction in their wake. But deep down, he never believed it himself. And why should he? He hadn't meant any of those apologies. He had no intention of making things right, of making amends. To him, sorry was hollow, a lifeline he clung to without any real effort to change.

The drinking only made it worse. Alcohol gave him an excuse, a way to justify his behaviour. "Sorry" was something he used to buy himself more time, a bandage he slapped on wounds that needed much deeper healing. And even when people stopped believing him, he kept using it, kept expecting that somehow the word alone would be enough.

But now, sitting at this table, sober and raw, he finally understands. An apology isn't the end of the journey; it's the start of something much harder: change. Words alone can't heal the wounds he's caused. People don't want his apologies anymore. They want proof—actions. They want to see the man he's trying to become, not the man who hides behind his past mistakes.

He knows this now. And for the first time, it terrifies him.

Sitting at the table, knowing that the people he's hurt don't want his words anymore, TJ knows they want truth, they want proof. He's come to understand that actions, not words, are the only way to rebuild trust. And yet, sorry still sticks to the roof of his mouth like a habit he can't quite shake.

He remembers all the times he's said it, sometimes not even believing it himself. He remembers the hollow apologies that slipped through his lips, and how powerless he felt each time they were met with scepticism. Years of lies and self-pity have taught him one thing: sorry is just the start.

But what about you? What do you think?

You've been here, haven't you? Maybe not in the same way, but you know what it's like to say sorry when, deep down, you know it's not enough. Maybe you've been on the receiving end, waiting for someone to change, to prove that their words were more than just empty promises. Or maybe, like me, you've been the one saying sorry, expecting it to make everything okay when you had no intention of backing it up with action.

How many times have you said sorry and known, in your heart, it wasn't enough? Think about it. Was it to a friend? A loved one? A parent? Did you expect them to forgive you just because you said the words? Maybe you meant it at the time. So, what did you do after? Did you change? Or did you go back to your old ways, expecting another sorry to cover up the damage?

That's the thing about sorry. It's not the end of something—it's the beginning. A promise that things will be different. But without action, it's meaningless. Just like I had to learn the hard way, so do you. If you've hurt people, if you've thrown around apologies like they're supposed to fix everything, ask yourself this: what do your actions look like afterward? Because what people remember is the actions, not the words.

Now, before we go any further, I need you to think about something. I told you in the last chapter that this book isn't just about me—it's about you too. And it is. So, if there's something in you that feels unsettled, if you've said sorry too many times without following through, maybe this is the time to reflect.

Where have words done the work of actions in your life? Do you think it's time to change that?"

TJ knows this all too well now. Deep down, in his heart and soul, he understands that it was never just about saying sorry. After years of drunkenness and broken promises, who could blame anyone for being sceptical? On its own, it's just a word—empty, unless backed by something more.

He remembers one time, years ago, when he was deep in his addiction. It was a typical night—too many drinks, too many reckless decisions. He'd lashed out at Frida, said things he couldn't take back, things that dug deep into her trust. The next morning, hungover and filled with regret, he had mumbled an apology. "I'm sorry," he had said, rubbing his temple as if that could somehow erase the damage.

But even as the words left his lips, he knew he wasn't ready to change. He wasn't ready to stop the drinking, the anger, the self-destruction. Frida had heard it all before. And though she'd nodded, TJ could see it in her eyes—she didn't believe him. She couldn't. Why would she? That apology, like so many before it, was just another empty promise.

And, just like that, nothing changed. He went back to his old ways, telling himself that sorry should have been enough, but deep down, he knew better. It wasn't sorry that would save him, it was action. It was showing her, day after day, that he could be the man she needed him to be.

People don't want to hear the same old apology. They need to see it, feel it in the actions that follow. They want proof that change is happening, that the person who hurt them is willing to go the extra mile to make things right. Amends aren't just about words; they're about consistent, genuine acts of goodwill. It's about showing up differently, again and again, until trust is slowly rebuilt.

So, maybe that's the real question for both of us, isn't it? Can we make our apologies real, not just with words but with actions? Can we start to show the people we've hurt that we've changed, not just say it? The time for words is over. Now it's time to act."

But the real question now looms larger than ever: is he willing? Willing to not only make amends the right way, but to face the consequences of his past, no matter what they might be? He's sober, yes. But sobriety is only the beginning. The real work starts with willingness.

And deep down, TJ wonders... Does he truly have it in him?

But here's the thing—what about you?

You've been following TJ's story, but let's pause for a second and think about yours.

Have you ever needed to make amends, felt the urgency to right your wrongs? But did you stop to consider the impact on those around you?

Think carefully. Would you rush in, driven by your own need for relief, without thinking about the harm it might cause? Step 9 reminds us that sometimes, making amends is about more than just clearing our conscience. It's about thinking of others, about doing what's right for them, not just what feels right for us.

So, are you willing? Not just to say sorry, but to do the real work. The careful work. The work that requires thought, consideration, and patience. The time for words is over. Now it's time to act.

WILLINGNESS IS THE KEY

Hi, guess who? Yeah, me again.

Willingness. It sounds so simple, doesn't it? Just a word, but within it lies the power to unlock a life of freedom or keep someone chained to their past. I understand this now. Willingness isn't just about wanting to change; it's about being ready to act on that desire. It's about doing the work, even when it's hard, even when it hurts.

For me, willingness becomes the turning point in my recovery. But it isn't just about my own sobriety anymore. I've realized something deeper—I can only keep what I have by giving it away. Every time I help someone else, I help myself. Every time I reach out to a struggling soul, my own burdens lighten.

But what about you? Where does willingness fit into your life? Is there something you've been holding back? Maybe it's the willingness to forgive someone, or perhaps it's the willingness to finally let go of a burden you've carried for too long.

Willingness is the key, yes, but it's also a challenge. It requires more than just a word—it demands action, and I for one know this. I feel it every day when I wake up, determined to give back what was so freely given to me. I can't do it alone, but with a willing heart, I've learned that I don't have to.

But one thing I wake up with every morning is gratitude. Gratitude to be alive. I wake up with tears in my eyes—not tears of sadness, not tears of self-pity, not tears of fear, and not tears of shame—but tears of knowing that I have a life beyond my wildest dreams. A life where I have choices.

Today, I have to be willing to put those choices into action, because actions speak volumes rather than words.

Gratitude isn't just about saying "thank you" for the life I have—it's about feeling it deeply, knowing that everything I do is a reflection of the willingness to change. Every breath, every step I take, is a gift. There were days when I couldn't see past my own pain, when I thought, my life would never amount to anything more than broken promises and shattered relationships. But today, I wake up grateful for the second chances I've been given, and for the fact that I can offer those chances to others.

Willingness and gratitude go hand in hand. Without gratitude, willingness falters. It's easy to say we're willing to change, willing to act, but without a heart full of gratitude, it becomes empty—a routine we follow without meaning. I've learned that true willingness comes from a place of humility, from understanding that I'm no longer in control of everything and that's okay. Because today, I don't have to be.

I wake up every morning with tears of joy because I realize I have something I never had before—freedom. Not the kind of freedom that means I can do whatever I want, but the kind of freedom that gives me choices. Real choices. The choice to be better, the choice to give back, the choice to live each day with purpose. But these choices mean nothing if I'm not willing to act on them. That's where willingness comes in—it's what turns those choices into reality.

Every day, I remind myself that willingness isn't a one-time decision. It's something I have to renew each morning. I have to wake up and ask myself: What am I willing to do today to keep this life I've been given? Am I willing to be honest? Am I willing to admit when I'm wrong? Am I willing to put others before myself, not out of obligation, but because I truly care? These are the questions that drive me forward, that make willingness more than just a word.

Gratitude gives me the strength to be willing.

When I remember how far I've come, the things I've survived, I realize that every moment is a chance to do better. To be better. And that's where the willingness comes in—to recognize the gift of life and make it count. To use my experiences, my pain, my victories, to help others find their own way.

Patience, tolerance, and understanding are imperative in a life of meaning, a life that goes somewhere. Without these, it's too easy to get caught up in frustration, to let anger or resentment take over. Patience is about giving time—for yourself and others—to grow, to change, and to heal. It's not about rushing the process but trusting that things will unfold as they're meant to.

Tolerance means accepting people as they are, flaws and all. It doesn't mean tolerating harmful behaviour, but rather understanding that everyone is on their own journey, facing their own battles. We can't control how others act or react, but we can choose how we respond—with compassion instead of judgment.

And then there's understanding. It's the foundation of everything. To live a life with meaning, we need to seek to understand before we judge, before we react. Understanding brings empathy, and empathy brings connection. Without it, we're isolated in our own pain, stuck in a loop of misunderstanding and anger.

These three—patience, tolerance, and understanding—aren't just virtues; they're essential tools. They help us build relationships that matter. They help us find meaning even in the most difficult times. And they help us stay grounded when life throws challenges our way.

Look, I get it. Maybe you've been through your own storms—maybe not like mine, but ones that still left you feeling broken. I know exactly what that's like. I know what it's like to wake up and feel like everything is shattered, like no amount of sorry or regret can put it back together. You might feel like you've lost pieces of yourself along the way, and it hurts a great deal.

There's a weight in your chest that sometimes feels like it's too much to carry. I know that feeling. I've been there, saw it and although I can still struggle in certain areas, with a little willingness I get through it a day at a time. There've been times when I didn't think I'd survive another day. The fear, the shame, the loneliness—it all builds up until you feel like there's no way out. But there is. I'm standing here, telling you there is.

I'm not just talking about hope or some distant idea of happiness. I'm talking about the real, raw stuff—the kind of love that you find when you least expect it. The kind that pulls you out of the darkness, not because everything magically gets better, but because you start to understand that you're not alone. I've had my share of pain, and I've been through things that tore me apart, but you know what? I learned that in the middle of all that mess, there's still love.

There's still light.

So, if you're sitting there listening to me and you somewhat feel like no one understands, trust me, I understand. I've faced my own demons, and some days they still try to claw their way back in. But what keeps me going is knowing that I don't have to fight alone anymore—and neither do you.

It's not all about me. It's about you, too. I get it, easier said than done, right? Maybe you're sitting there, reading this, thinking...

"Yeah, that sounds nice, but how am I supposed to keep going?"

I've been there, done it and I've worn that T-shirt more times than I can count. But here's the thing: If I can keep going—through all of it—then maybe you can, too. What if today is the day you find that little bit of willingness? Come on, you can do it.

At least try...

It doesn't have to take flashing lights or an astounding miracle.

Be the miracle.

You don't have to solve everything today, but wouldn't you agree that at least you need to be willing? Because without willingness, nothing moves. It's not about perfection, it's about showing up, putting in the effort today, even when you don't know what tomorrow will bring.

Yesterday's history. Tomorrow's a mystery. All we truly have is to-day. Just focus on what you can do right now. Willingness is about taking small steps, putting in the effort today, even if you're not sure where it will lead. It's not about perfection, but about trying. Because in those small steps today, you lay the foundation for incredible change tomorrow.

The prayer is the asking. The meditation is the listening. And I'm not talking about fancy rituals or hours spent trying to quiet your mind. Sometimes, it's just a few minutes—a moment of honesty with yourself, a moment of surrender. That's how I started. Just a few words, admitting that I couldn't do this on my own. Because I can't.

I've said it before, and I'll say it again: I can't do this on my own.

But what about you? Do you think you can? Do you think you can change or work on what needs changing all by yourself? Or do you feel like maybe, just maybe, you need something more? Maybe it's a friend, a partner, or even something deeper, something within. Could it be that the help you need goes beyond what you can see? Something higher, something greater, a force that's been waiting for you to reach out?

It's not as simple as someone else saying they believe in you; it's about you believing in yourself.

So where do you start? Start small. Start with today. Maybe that means taking a few minutes to sit with yourself. Maybe it means reaching out to someone who's been where you are. Maybe it's as simple as saying...

"I don't know what to do, but I'm willing to try."

That's all it takes—a little willingness.

But what if you're struggling to find that willingness? I've been there, too. Whenever I felt weak in spirit, like I couldn't muster the strength to keep going, I'd remind myself of one thing: Take yourself out of yourself and go help someone else. There's something powerful in stepping outside of your own pain and giving to others. It doesn't have to be big. Maybe it's as simple as checking in on someone, offering a hand, or just being there to listen.

The only way I found to build self-esteem was by doing the right thing, by thinking of somebody else without expecting anything in return. Not even a thank you. That's where selflessness comes in—because true selflessness is about thinking of ourselves less, not putting ourselves down, but shifting our focus to others. It's in those moments of giving, of stepping outside our own struggles, that we start to heal. And in that selfless action, we find strength we didn't know we had.

When you're struggling to find that willingness, remember that helping others can help you. It's a way to shift the focus, to stop the spiral of doubt and fear, and to realize that even in your weakest moments, you have something to give. And that's where healing starts—when you give, without expectation, without strings, you start to rebuild yourself from the inside out.

You have to be willing to try. To keep going. And when it gets hard—and it will—remember this: you're not alone. I'm here. I've been there. And I'm still here, still walking the path, still learning as I go. And if I can keep going, so can you. Come on, we'll do it together.

Because the truth is, life is messy. It's filled with ups and downs, with struggles and moments of doubt. But the one thing that keeps us moving forward is our willingness to keep trying, to keep showing up, even when we don't have all the answers. It's about taking things one day at a time, one step at a time, and trusting that if we're willing to stay in the fight, change will come.

You don't need to have all the answers. All you need is the willingness to try—to be open, to take that first step. And when it feels like too much, remember: you're not alone. I'm right here with you, walking beside you. Together, we'll keep going, step by step. But here's the real question: are you ready? Are you willing to take that step today? Because it starts with one small decision. Right now. Just for today. What will you do next?

FORGIVENESS

TJ sits quietly, the weight of the word forgiveness pressing heavily on his mind. It's a word people often throw around, but TJ knows it's a lot more complicated than that. Forgiveness doesn't come easily—not for others, and certainly not for himself. He's spent years carrying the burden of his own mistakes, thinking that seeking forgiveness from others was the only way to make things right.

But now, he's starting to realize something deeper. Forgiving others is impossible without first forgiving himself. How can he let go of the pain caused by others when he hasn't been able to release the weight of his own guilt? He knows now that forgiveness isn't just a word; it's a process, and like everything else in recovery, it starts with a willingness to try.

TJ doesn't need anyone else's approval to move forward. He thought he did for a long time—waiting for validation, for someone to tell him it was okay to forgive himself. But now, sitting here in the quiet, he realizes that the only approval he needs is already his. God's. And in that realization, he finds the strength to begin the process of forgiving himself.

But the thing is, forgiveness isn't just about trying—it's about learning. TJ has had to learn to forgive, and it hasn't been easy. He thinks about what his higher power did for him, how He willingly laid down His life, bled all over that cross, and died for TJ's sins. And every time TJ reflects on that, he feels a sense of deep gratitude. If Jesus could make that choice—to become less, to give everything—surely TJ can find it within himself to forgive others.

Yet, as much as that thought softens the blow, it doesn't make forgiveness easy. It's not a simple decision, and it's certainly not something that happens overnight. TJ realizes that forgiveness is a process, one that takes time and effort, and sometimes, it takes much more than just one prayer or one moment of clarity. It takes reminding himself, over and over again, that forgiveness isn't just about the other person—it's about freeing himself from the chains of anger and resentment.

When TJ thinks about forgiving others, he also reflects on how God forgave him. God's grace was given freely, without hesitation, and without holding anything back. If God can forgive him, in all his brokenness, in all his mistakes, then shouldn't he be able to extend that same grace to others? But even knowing that, it's not always easy. Forgiveness, after all, is more than just a word. It's a choice—a choice that TJ has to make each day.

And that's the thing about forgiveness. It doesn't happen all at once. It's not a one-and-done kind of thing. Sometimes, forgiveness takes more than one day at a time—it takes a minute at a time. There are days when TJ has to remind himself to forgive again and again. He might pray the prayer and say the words, but he finds that some days he has to forgive a hundred times, especially when the wounds run deep. And that's okay. Forgiveness, TJ has learned, isn't about the other person's response. It's about his own heart, his own peace.

The truth is, TJ doesn't need anyone else's approval to forgive. He used to think he did. He used to wait for some kind of acknowledgment or validation from the people around him, but now he knows better. He already has God's approval, and that's enough. That's everything. God's grace covers all, and that's what gives him the strength to keep forgiving, even when it's hard, even when it feels impossible.

TJ realizes something else: forgiveness isn't just about letting go of what others have done. It's about letting go of the weight he's been carrying. If he can't forgive them, how can he expect to move forward? How can he expect to truly forgive himself? Forgiveness, he knows, isn't just about letting go of the past—it's about clearing the way forward. Without forgiveness, the weight of anger and guilt only drags him back, holds him down. But with forgiveness, TJ can move forward with a lighter heart, with the freedom to live his life fully.

Deep down, TJ knows this: holding on to resentment will only keep him stuck. Without forgiveness, the path forward is blocked. He has to release the past, for his own sake. Forgiveness, he knows, isn't just about letting go of the past—it's about clearing the way forward. Without forgiveness, the weight of anger and guilt only drags him down, holds him back. But with forgiveness, TJ can move forward with a lighter heart, with a free will to live his life fully.

Yet, forgiveness isn't a one-time thing for TJ. Every day, he has to forgive two people who, in his heart, have caused him the deepest pain. One of them is Uncle Rich, the man whose presence haunted his childhood. The things that happened back then, the words and actions that left scars—TJ has to confront those memories every single day. And every single day, he has to choose to forgive.

The other is the man in Bristol, the one who attacked him without mercy. That moment, that act of violence, left physical and emotional wounds that run deep. Forgiving that man feels impossible some days. But TJ knows that if he holds on to the anger, to the hate, it will only chain him to the past. So, he tries. Every day, he tries to forgive, even when it feels like the hardest thing in the world.

Because deep down, TJ knows this: if he can't forgive them, how can he expect to be forgiven himself? He's learned that forgiveness isn't about excusing what they did—it's about freeing himself from the prison of resentment. It's about choosing peace over pain, love over anger.

And so, with each new day, TJ wakes up and makes the choice to forgive, again and again. It's not always easy. In fact, some days, it feels like the hardest thing he'll ever do. But he knows it's the only way forward.

After all, forgiveness is not just about them—it's about him, too.

So, each day, TJ makes the choice to forgive. It's not a grand gesture. It's not something that always feels monumental. But it's a choice he makes nonetheless. He forgives, not because the other person deserves it, but because he deserves the peace that comes with it. And in those moments, when forgiveness feels like an uphill battle, he remembers what his higher power did for him, and he realizes that the power to forgive is already within him. It's just a matter of being willing to let it go, one moment at a time.

Forgiveness opens a door, not just to healing but to something much deeper—something spiritual. TJ has come to understand that true forgiveness is an act of the soul, not bound by rules or rituals. It's not about religion; it's about something far greater, something that goes beyond what people tried to teach him as a child.

For many, Jesus, that name comes with baggage, with memories of rules and expectations. But TJ has learned that his higher power wasn't about rules at all. He was and indeed is all about love. Pure, unconditional, life-giving love. He wasn't bound by religion; He broke through it, offering a relationship instead of a set of rules. And that's what TJ has come to realize—that this isn't about religion, it's about connection, about a love that doesn't condemn but heals.

As TJ reflects on his journey, he knows now that Jesus was always there, not with judgment but with open arms, waiting. The forever hurting healer who took on the weight of the world's pain, including TJ's. And now, TJ is ready to walk forward with Him, no longer running, but embracing the love that was there all along.

THE FOREVER HURTING HEALER

TJ's thoughts drift to the quiet moments—the ones when the world seemed to crumble around him, yet something, someone, always held him together. It wasn't the loud voices of judgment, or the people who had tried to teach him about rules and religion. No, it was something softer, something deeper. A presence that never left him, no matter how far he ran.

In those moments, when TJ thought he was all alone, he now sees the truth. He wasn't alone. Jesus, the forever hurting healer, had been there all along, carrying TJ's pain, even when TJ didn't realize it. It wasn't until now, after surrendering and learning to forgive, that TJ could see it clearly—the love that had been with him through it all.

TJ often reflects on the Bible—not just as a collection of stories or lessons, but as the living, breathing Word of God. It's not a book that contains God's words; it is God's Word, alive and constant. And much like the Bible, TJ's life, through all its ups and downs, has been a testament to God's enduring presence and grace.

He remembers the day he was saved, when everything seemed to shift, though at the time, he hadn't fully grasped the depth of what that meant. Looking back now, he sees that God didn't just step into his life—He stepped into TJ's future, correcting the mistakes of his past, allowing him to live freely in the present. It's a truth that resonates deeply within him now, especially after coming through the trials of addiction and self-doubt.

In the same way that God gave Noah a vision—a purpose to build the Ark—TJ realizes he, too, was given a vision. A vision that, for years, he shrugged off, not believing it could ever come to pass. Like many, he spent much of his life wandering, wondering, "What's my purpose? What am I supposed to be doing?" But the answer was always there, waiting for him to embrace it. And now, after years of resistance, TJ understands.

God had shown him a purpose long ago, one that seemed impossible in the midst of his struggles. He was told to write a book, but TJ thought it was ludicrous. How could he write anything when he struggled even to spell? It felt like a pipe dream—unreachable, too far beyond his grasp. But God's vision isn't bound by our limitations.

There was more to the plan. TJ was also shown that before he could write, he needed to get his driver's license. The purpose wasn't just to write; it was to move forward in life, to take practical steps. Years later, when TJ finally embraced that vision, he realized that God had already put the pieces in place. He went to college, passing English, math, and I.T. qualifications. Ironically, the college even offered him twenty free driving lessons, just as he was told. The vision, so far-fetched in the beginning, started to come together in ways TJ couldn't have imagined.

The world celebrates its actors and singers, worshipping them for their talents. TJ used to look at them the same way, thinking that their fame was something to admire. But now, he knows the truth. Jesus wasn't a singer or an actor, yet He sang the most incredible song into TJ's heart—and into the hearts of every believer. His love is deeper than any applause, more real than any fame.

God doesn't need a stage to be remembered. He doesn't need adoration to make His presence known. He's already written His name on the hearts of those who are willing to receive Him, and what He offers is a gift more precious than anything money could buy. It's freedom, freedom too—true freedom. A life beyond daylight, beyond fear, beyond anything this world could offer. A life that stretches into eternity.

And God did this, and continues to do this, for one reason alone: because He loves. That love was there for TJ even when TJ didn't know it, and now, after everything, TJ is ready to accept and embrace it fully.

As TJ sits in quiet reflection, the memories of his out-of-body experiences flood his mind—moments where he was teetering on the edge of life and death. The first time it happened, he had overdosed, and everything went black. But then, he felt himself being lifted out of his body, taken to a rocky, desolate place. In the midst of the darkness, there stood his higher power, not with judgment or anger, but with compassion. TJ remembers how his higher power didn't challenge God, but simply asked for him. "He's already prayed the prayer," He said. "He's already mine."

At the time, TJ had been in his twenties, still deep in addiction, and didn't fully understand what was happening. He had prayed the prayer of salvation but was drowning in alcohol and chaos. He couldn't yet comprehend that his life was being shaped, that God had already begun moulding him, even when he felt lost. It was in that rocky place that his higher power had took hold of him, laying the foundation for the transformation that would take years to fully unfold.

The second time was during the Bristol attack—a brutal, senseless act of violence that left TJ battered physically and emotionally. As he drifted into unconsciousness, he had another out-of-body experience. This time, he found himself on an island, surrounded by a vast ocean, and in the distance, he saw a rollercoaster. The twists and turns mirrored the chaos of his life—the highs and devastating lows that he had endured. Yet, even as he watched the rollercoaster of his life go upside down, TJ felt a calm presence beside him. His higher power was there, watching with him, waiting.

But there was more.

In that moment, although he didn't realise at the time, TJ saw something else—an Alcoholics Anonymous meeting, a gathering of people who, like him, were searching for healing. He didn't fully understand it at the time, but his higher power had shown him the way forward.

"Stay here, until I call you home," his friend had told him.

It wasn't just a command to find sobriety—it was a call to remain on the path, to stay sober, until his journey in this world was complete. It wasn't about waiting for the right moment to act—it was about staying true to the path, day by day, moment by moment, until the final call. TJ didn't realize the depth of that message then, but looking back now, he understands that God wasn't just asking for willingness. He was asking for commitment—for a life dedicated to walking that path of healing, until the day he was called home.

It's the side of himself that TJ had long refused to look at that ruled him. He had spent years running from his own darkness, afraid that if he looked too closely, he would never escape it. But now, as he sits and reflects, he understands that true freedom can only be found by confronting the very shadows he once fled. To heal his mind and heart, TJ knows he must be willing to face the parts of himself that terrify him. This is the road to freedom—walking into the darkness to find the light, stepping into his deepest fears to discover peace.

He begins to see that the secrets he has kept hidden, the guilt he has carried for so long, were chains that bound him to his past. But by revealing those secrets—by speaking them aloud and releasing their hold—he can finally change the way he thinks, and in turn, change the way he lives. TJ knows that his thoughts have the power to shape his future. What he will be tomorrow is determined by what he chooses to think and believe today.

The journey hasn't been easy, but the further TJ walks down the path of forgiveness, the clearer it becomes. The book of his life has always been about freedom in Christ—freedom born not from running away from pain, but from embracing it. It's a story of love, redemption, and healing, not just for him but for those who have been impacted by his actions. It's a story of how Jesus, the forever hurting healer, has guided him through every moment of darkness, never leaving his side, even when TJ couldn't see Him.

This realization is powerful.

Forgiveness is no longer just an act—it's a way of living, a daily choice. It's not about excusing the past but releasing it, finding peace through the acceptance that he is already forgiven by God. The darkness, the mistakes, the guilt—they no longer have control over him. Christ's love has redeemed those broken pieces, making TJ whole again. And as he moves forward, he understands that this journey isn't just about himself—it's about sharing that freedom and love with others, guiding them towards the same light he's found.

TJ reflects on all that he's been through, the forgiveness, the healing, and the moments where his higher power showed him the way. But deep down, there's still a question that lingers, one that he hasn't fully answered yet:

Is he ready to carry the love and forgiveness he's been shown into the world, to those who may never ask for it? Is he willing to be the light for others, just as Christ has been for him?

Only time will tell if TJ can live up to the vision he's been given. The next steps of his journey remain unwritten, and he knows that his story is far from over.

THE AWAKENING

TJ doesn't recognize the exact moment it happens, but somewhere along the way, something inside him shifts. It's not a lightning bolt of clarity or a dramatic epiphany—it's more like a quiet, steady awakening that unfolds over time. And it's not just TJ who notices it; his sister, partner, and friends all see the change in subtle ways. They recognize a transformation in him—a man once volatile and lost, now different.

This awakening isn't like the fleeting spiritual experiences TJ encountered in the past. He has had moments of transcendence before, times that felt like touching something holy, but those experiences were temporary. A spiritual awakening runs deeper. It's not just a passing moment; it's a transformation that takes root and changes how he lives.

It's evident in the way he responds rather than reacts. The old TJ would have blown up, shouted, or lashed out. He would have turned to a bottle to drown his feelings. But now, there's a pause—a breath. He takes a moment to consider. Instead of reacting in anger, he chooses patience. Instead of letting frustration control him, he embraces understanding. This change doesn't stem from one big decision; it's the result of daily work—the forgiveness he's offered and the grace he's accepted.

His sister, always quick to call out his temper, is the first to notice. "You're different, Tea Jay," she tells him with quiet amazement. "You're not the same guy who used to lose it over everything."

His partner notices it too. She sees how TJ remains calm in situations where he once would have slammed the door or driven off in frustration. Now, he sits down, takes a breath, and talks things through. She sees the peace in his eyes that wasn't there before.

Even his friends notice the difference. Those who had known him during his darkest moments see something new. It's not just that TJ is sober; it's that he's awake—awake to life and to himself.

TJ wonders, "How did this happen?" This spiritual awakening didn't come with fanfare or grand revelation. It arrived gradually, in small moments of daily commitment to living differently. It came through self-reflection, making amends, and choosing forgiveness over resentment. Now, that work is showing in ways TJ never anticipated.

For TJ, this awakening isn't just about understanding how to live differently; it's about the peace that accompanies it. He feels more at ease in his own skin and more comfortable in situations that would have once triggered him. He finds himself responding with a calm that surprises him. Where he once reacted with anger or defensiveness, now there's a pause, a breath, a moment of clarity before he speaks or acts.

Spiritual awakening isn't confined to any one religion; it isn't about following strict rules to avoid punishment. TJ knows that across the world's religions, many share common threads—ideas of fire and brimstone, warnings of damnation, and pressure to be good to secure a place in heaven. But that's not what spirituality is about. And it's certainly not what Christianity is truly about.

For TJ, Christianity isn't a "better" group of rules compared to other faiths. It's not about following dos and don'ts to tick boxes and evade consequences. Instead, it's about transformation—real change from the inside out. It's about giving when it feels hardest to give and loving when it's most difficult to love. The true blessing comes not from simply loving those closest to us but from showing kindness and compassion to strangers—the ones who need help but might never be able to repay it.

Religion, in its many forms, can sometimes devolve into scare-mongering—doing good simply to avoid bad outcomes. Many faiths, intentionally or unintentionally, can focus on escaping punishment or earning salvation. But TJ has learned that his journey through Christianity isn't about fear or obligation. It's about freedom—freedom to give without expectation, to love without conditions, and to live in a way that reflects the selfless love he believes Jesus embodies.

The heart of what TJ is trying to express isn't to insist that anyone must adopt Christianity; that is a personal choice. Instead, he invites people to live a little kinder, love a little deeper, and be more willing to help, even when there's nothing to gain. To TJ, spirituality is about paying it forward and creating small ripples of kindness that spread far beyond the moment. It's about actions, not rules. It's about understanding that every act of love, no matter how small, contributes to a greater good.

For TJ, this is the awakening—not a sudden, blinding moment of revelation, but a gradual unfolding of understanding. It's not about judgment or fire and brimstone. It's about showing up every day with a willing heart—willing to give, serve, and love.

This isn't a sign of weakness but strength. "Responding, not react-ing, that's the difference," he thinks. The awakening has empowered him to step outside himself, to see situations from a higher perspective. It's not about suppressing emotions but choosing how to direct them. In many ways, it's about control—but not in the way he once thought of it. It's not about forcing things to go his way; it's about knowing when to surrender and when to stand firm.

In the past, TJ's selfishness was all-consuming. He only thought of himself—his needs, desires, and pain. Everything revolved around his suffering. But with this awakening comes a profound shift in focus. He learns that selflessness isn't about losing himself in others but about giving freely, without expectation. By helping others, he also helps himself.

He finds himself willing to give more of his time and energy, not just to those close to him but to strangers—anyone in need. It's no longer a burden or obligation; it's a joy. "I don't do this because I have to," TJ reminds himself. "I do this because I want to." The beauty of this awakening lies not in grand gestures but in little moments—quiet acts of kindness that matter most. A smile to someone who's struggling, a few words of encouragement to someone who's lost, a simple gesture of empathy—these fill his days now.

And the people around him notice. His sister, who once braced for his outbursts, now trusts him in a way she never could before. His partner, who had spent years waiting for the other shoe to drop, now looks at him with calm and stability. They see it in his actions, in the way he moves through the world with a newfound purpose.

This awakening has also brought a deep sense of responsibility. TJ knows he can't take his sobriety or peace for granted. Every day is a gift, but it's also a challenge. He understands that he can only keep what he has by giving it away. Helping others isn't just a side effect of his recovery; it's central to it. He knows that by reaching out to those who are still struggling, he ensures his own growth and continued awakening.

But this doesn't mean TJ lets others walk all over him. His new selflessness comes with boundaries. He's not afraid to say no when needed or to stand firm when someone crosses a line. This isn't about being a martyr or a doormat—it's about being real, about authenticity. His willingness to help others doesn't mean compromising his values or letting others take advantage of his kindness. It means being there, fully present, without losing sight of who he is.

As much as TJ has awakened to a new way of life, he knows it doesn't make him immune to pain or struggle. One person, in particular, keeps him up at night—his brother, Jay. For years, TJ has watched Jay waste away, consumed by his battles. He's tried to help, to offer a way out, but there's only so much he can do. Jay is sick, not just in body but in soul, and despite TJ's pleading, Jay isn't ready to accept the help that could save him.

TJ's heart aches as he watches Jay's condition deteriorate. Diabetes has already claimed one of Jay's toes, and the disease is creeping through the rest of his body. Jay looks frail—a shadow of the man TJ once knew—and every time TJ visits, he can't shake the feeling that time is running out. It scares him. But as much as TJ wants to fix things, to save his brother, he knows one undeniable truth: he's powerless over people, places, and things. And that's the hardest part of the awakening.

Just because TJ has found peace in his own life doesn't mean he can force others to do the same. It's a bitter pill to swallow, watching someone you love struggle when the answer seems so clear. But TJ knows that, like he did, Jay has to find his own way. All he can do is offer love, support, and hope that one day Jay will ask for help. As much as TJ has awakened, he's still human. He feels the pain, fear, and sadness. He's learning to accept life on life's terms—recognizing that part of this spiritual awakening involves understanding that everyone has their own path to walk.

As TJ reflects on this journey, he realizes that the awakening didn't happen all at once. It wasn't a single moment of clarity that changed everything. Instead, it was a series of small shifts and choices that eventually led him to where he is now. Every time he chose to respond instead of react, every time he chose kindness over anger, and every time he prioritized someone else's needs—those were the moments that shaped him and brought him to this place of peace and purpose.

Now, standing on the other side of that journey, TJ understands something fundamental: a spiritual awakening isn't about perfection. It's about progress. It's about choosing, day after day, to live in alignment with his values and to be the person he was always meant to be.

For TJ, the spiritual awakening he's experiencing isn't tied to rigid structures of organized religion. It's not about rules or doctrines. His journey isn't about pushing a religious agenda or insisting that others must be "saved" in the traditional sense. Instead, it's about something deeper—an awakening of the soul, a spiritual realization that transcends any single belief system. It's about connection—to himself, to others, and to something greater.

Spirituality, TJ has come to understand, is a deeply personal journey. It's not about fire and brimstone or following a set of rules to avoid punishment. It's about living in alignment with the deepest truths of the human experience—love, compassion, understanding, and forgiveness. For TJ, these elements come together to create real, lasting change in his life.

What TJ has found is that spirituality isn't confined to one path; it isn't exclusive to any particular faith. It's about transformation—awakening to who you truly are and who you're meant to be. For TJ, his spiritual awakening means moving away from the destructive patterns that once controlled him—addiction, anger, fear—and stepping into a life of purpose, service, and giving back.

This book isn't about imposing any single belief on the reader. It's not a call for people to adopt specific religious practices or believe in a particular doctrine. Rather, it's a story about redemption, healing, and overcoming the darkest parts of oneself to embrace the light. It's about the universal human experiences of pain, loss, and struggle—and how, with the right mindset and support, anyone can rise from those depths.

As TJ continues his path, he realizes that his spiritual journey is about being real, helping others genuinely, and living with kindness and integrity. It's not about preaching salvation through fear or condemnation, but finding peace through love, forgiveness, and selflessness. TJ's awakening is a story for anyone seeking transformation—whether they come from a religious background or not. It's about becoming the best version of oneself and learning to keep what you have by giving it away, by helping others.

"Only me again, TJ. Yes, I'm talking to you—the one who's been taking the time to get to know me.

I have asked you before, but this time it's different.

I've asked you this before, but let's take a moment. Are you ready? Ready to face what's been waiting for you? Or maybe you've already started the journey. Maybe you've taken the first step. But here's the real question—are you willing to see where it takes you, to keep moving forward, and see what unfolds?

Change is scary. Trust me, I know. But what's scarier? Staying the same. I've been there, stuck, afraid to move, afraid to face what's next.

But I'm here, still walking this path with you by my side, still learning, still growing. And if I can do it, so can you.

All right, so here we are. What next?

Maybe there's more to dig into—about you, about me. There's no rush, no pressure. The light's been here the whole time, just waiting for us to notice. So, what do you say? Let's dive a little deeper, see where this ride takes us.

And don't worry—you're not on your own in this. We've come this far together, and there's no turning back now. The best part? We're just getting started. So, what do you think? You ready for what's next?

"

LEAVE OUT VIOLENT EMOTIONS

F orgiveness, Acceptance, Insight, Trust, and Hope

Let me tell you how I feel about love and faith.

Where does faith come from? For me, it is the only place I've ever found real peace. Not fleeting or superficial, but the kind of peace that comes from within—quiet, powerful. Faith has always been the guiding light I struggled to find but so desperately needed. It really challenged me, and it still challenges me. Yes, it is the thing, the very thing that has always saved me.

Reflecting on my childhood, I remember moments of happiness overshadowed by volatility. Growing up in a household rife with alcoholism, I learned early on that love was often complicated. My mother, who was a recovering alcoholic before she died, provided moments of warmth, but there was also chaos in the house. The violence loomed large, and I experienced childhood abuse that left deep scars. Uncle Rich brought confusion and fear with his unsettling behaviours. He loved us in his own special way, but it was always in the wrong way, and it was a love tinged with discomfort and misunderstanding.

In contrast, Uncle Rob was the embodiment of kindness. He was a father figure who offered protection and affection when I needed it most. He was a beacon of love in my life. Although Uncle Rob died a couple of years ago, his memory remains a source of comfort for me. I recall the chaos that erupted when my mother left cigarettes and a lighter in plain view. I picked up the lighter and set some tissue on fire under her bed, not fully understanding the consequences. The house went up in flames, and I was just five years old, feeling the immense weight of abandonment when I was separated from my sister and thrust into a children's home.

At home, I often asked for simple things, like an apple, only to be reminded that I should feel free to take what I needed. "You don't have to ask," my mother would say. But home was a concept I struggled to grasp; love was a language I had never been taught.

As I grew older, the cycle continued. Drinking became my escape, and all the places I ran to felt like the solution. But the truth was—and sometimes still is—the problem lay within me.

Without the tools to express or receive love, I easily find myself adrift, full of fear and unable to love myself. The absence of examples for healthy love leaves me feeling empty, caught in a circle of self-doubt and frustration.

But here's the difference: I notice now. I see the flare-ups of emotion for what they are—a reflection of past fears and insecurities. The real challenge isn't just stopping emotions; it's about staying stopped. It's not about never feeling anger or frustration; it's about recognizing when those feelings arise and choosing to breathe through them, to deal with them constructively.

This time, when the feelings arise, I try to take a step back. I realize I'm only as good as I am today—I haven't had a character transplant. So, I allow myself to breathe deeply and attempt to let those feelings pass. The key difference this time? I can identify my part in things, and I understand it's not about eliminating emotions, but about learning how to respond rather than react.

Now, let me ask you: What do faith and love mean to you? Just something to think about as you read on.

For me, it has been and is a journey—a constant companion that continues to guide me through whatever darkness life throws my way. When I felt lost, faith provided a flicker of hope. It asked me to trust in something greater than myself, to embrace the unknown and find strength in vulnerability.

There were times when faith felt adrift, but today it's like a lifeline. I remember sitting alone in a crowded room, feeling invisible, my heart heavy with despair. In those moments, I learned to reach out—not just to others, but to the very essence of my faith. I asked myself, "What do I believe in?" and found solace in the answers that surfaced from within.

Just ask yourself...

Have you experienced moments where faith helped you overcome challenges? When was the last time you felt that spark of belief in yourself?

I'm inviting you to take a moment and reflect on your own journey. If it feels right, jot down a thought or two.

Faith is about progress, not perfection. It's about-facing challenges with love and selflessness, without expecting anything in return. That's how real relationships grow—especially when both people are walking the same path.

So, how can we cultivate faith in our daily lives?

For me, it's about small acts of kindness, both to myself and to others. It's about being present, practicing gratitude, and finding joy in simple moments. When I make the conscious choice to show up for myself, I invite faith to flourish.

As I reflect on my journey, I realize that true faith, the kind that sustains me through life's trials, comes from a deep-rooted belief in something greater than myself. The Bible teaches that faith is the assurance of things hoped for, the conviction of things not seen. This understanding of faith has been pivotal in my recovery. It reminds me that while I may not always see the path ahead, I can trust in the journey that unfolds.

Faith is not merely a passive feeling; it's an active choice to believe that God has a plan for me, even when times are tough. It's a reassurance that I am not alone in my struggles. The promises found in Scripture speak to the power of faith in transforming our lives. For instance, Philippians 4:13 reminds me, "I can do all things through Christ who strengthens me." This is not just a verse; it's a declaration of possibility—a mantra I hold onto when challenges arise.

Through my faith, I've learned to embrace acceptance. I've accepted that my past doesn't define my future and that every day is a new opportunity for growth. This acceptance is grounded in love—unconditional love for myself and others. I've come to understand that love is not a finite resource; it multiplies as I share it.

As I continue this journey, I see that my faith has cultivated a sense of hope within me. Hope is what fuels my willingness to put in the hard work required for recovery. It's the belief that no matter how deep the wounds of my past, healing is possible. Each step I take is guided by faith—a faith built on hard work, constructive effort, and the simple principle of living one day at a time.

So, let me ask you:

Wait a second—how rude of me! I've been talking to you all this time, and I haven't even asked your name.

How can we be on this journey together if I don't even know who you are? Yes, you, the one who's been walking beside me through all of this.

My name's TJ... what's yours?

Let me ask you...

How does faith manifest in your life? Do you see it as a guiding force that shapes your actions and decisions? Reflecting on your own experiences, how has faith played a role in your journey?

As I continue to navigate this journey, I hold onto the belief that faith will always be a guiding light. It encourages me to love a little deeper and live a little more authentically.

And if there's one thing I hope to offer, it's this: if I can help anyone—whether you're struggling with mental health, alcoholism, addiction, or any other challenge in life—that is my only aim. This isn't a self-help book, but if sharing my experiences can help, then it's been worth it. I've engaged with you throughout this journey, and I hope that in some way, my words have offered comfort, connection, or hope.

So, I ask you again: Are you ready to embrace what's waiting for you? Are you ready to let go of what's holding you back and step into the life that's been calling your name all along?

I wrote this book not just to pass a message of hope, but to invite you to join me on a broad highway to a new freedom.

Are you willing and able to take the plunge?

The door's narrow, but it's still open.

THE LIGHT BEYOND THE DARKNESS

A s I sit here reflecting on my journey, the concept of light fills my thoughts. In a world where darkness often looms large, faith has illuminated my path—a flicker of hope in moments of despair.

My life has been a tapestry of change, woven together by the lessons I've learned along the way. Each struggle has been a thread, reminding me of the resilience within me. I've come to understand that true strength isn't the absence of fear but the courage to face it head-on.

I am profoundly grateful for those who have walked alongside me. Uncle Rob, with his unwavering kindness, was a beacon of love when I needed it most. He taught me that love isn't just a word; it's an action—a commitment to being there for others. His lessons echo in my heart, guiding my interactions today.

Alongside Uncle Rob's lessons, my partner has transformed my understanding of love. Her unconditional support has shown me that love can heal old wounds and foster growth, illuminating my life with warmth and compassion. In her presence, I have found not just a partner but a fellow traveller on this journey toward healing.

There were moments when I felt like I couldn't carry the weight on my own. But in those darkest times, a community of faith stepped in, offering more than just words—they lifted my family and me when we were struggling, reminding me that grace comes in many forms, sometimes through unexpected hands.

Reflecting on my past, I see how faith has played a pivotal role in shaping who I am today. It has challenged me, pushed me to grow, and guided me toward healing. I remember the lessons from the Bible, reminding me that faith is the assurance of things hoped for, the conviction of things not seen. This understanding of faith has been my guiding light, illuminating even the darkest corners of my life.

Now, let me ask you—what does faith mean to you? Can you see the light within yourself, shining even when times are tough? Or does it feel just beyond your reach, hidden in the shadows?

I invite you to reflect on your own journey. Look in the mirror and see the strength that lies within—or is there a light far beyond any darkness, waiting to be uncovered?

As I continue to navigate this journey, I hold onto the belief that faith will always be my guiding light. It encourages me to love deeper and live more authentically. I know that challenges may lie ahead, but I also know that I am not alone.

This journey isn't just about me; it's about each of us, together, moving toward our own light.

Reflecting on this journey of change that has brought me here, I can't help but feel a profound sense of gratitude. Change isn't always easy; it's often fraught with discomfort and uncertainty. Yet, through certain challenges, I've found resilience I never thought I had. The moments that once felt overwhelming have become stepping stones toward a brighter future.

I am especially grateful for the support of my partner, who has been my rock throughout this journey. Her unwavering belief in me has been a constant reminder of the power of love and faith. She encourages me to pursue my dreams, even when I doubt myself. This relationship has taught me the beauty of vulnerability and the strength that comes from being open to love.

As I also reflect a little further on my journey, I cannot forget the unwavering support of my sister, Lacey. She has been a constant source of strength, encouraging me through my darkest days and celebrating my victories with genuine joy. Her belief in me has helped illuminate my path, reminding me that family is a pillar of support. I am profoundly grateful for her presence in my life, just as I am thankful for the love of my wife, my guardian, and my faith in Jesus, who guides me daily.

Yet, as I stand here, illuminated by this light I've fought so hard to find, I realize that the journey is far from over—for both of us. We're just beginning to scratch the surface of what lies ahead. I can feel the pull of new adventures waiting on the horizon, and I hope you'll join me in uncovering the mysteries that await.

The people I've met throughout my AA journey have played a pivotal role in my recovery as well.

My sponsor has provided invaluable guidance and wisdom, helping me understand myself and the world around me. The support within this community has shown me the importance of connection and accountability. It reinforces the idea that it's not all about me; it's about us—lifting one another up as we navigate the road to recovery together. My past may be marked by mistakes, but I've learned that they don't define me. Instead, they serve as reminders of how far I've come and the lessons I've embraced.

Through this ongoing journey, I've come to understand that faith is not just a concept; it's a living, breathing part of my existence. It fuels my desire to help others and share my experiences.

In the grand tapestry of life, every thread matters. Each moment of joy, sorrow, love, and pain contributes to the whole. It's a reminder that while we all have our unique stories, we are interconnected. Our shared experiences bind us together, allowing us to find strength in one another.

As I prepare to conclude this chapter of my life, I hold on to the belief that my journey is just beginning. With faith as my guiding light, I'm excited for the possibilities that lie ahead. Each of us, with our unique stories, contributes to a beautiful tapestry of life, woven together by our experiences, struggles, and triumphs.

Let's embrace our journeys with open hearts, supporting one another as we navigate the complexities of life. Together, we can illuminate the darkness and celebrate the light within each of us. And as I stand at the threshold of new adventures, I can't help but feel that this is just the beginning.

What other mysteries await us on this journey?

Printed in Great Britain
by Amazon

54736403R00158